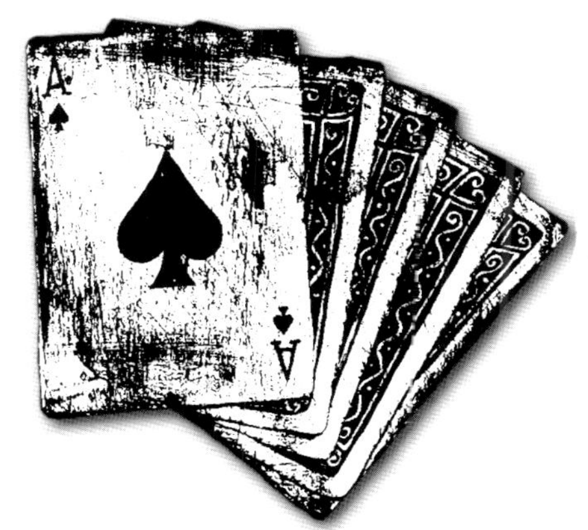

Readers, Advisors, and Storefront Churches

Renée Stout

A mid-career retrospective

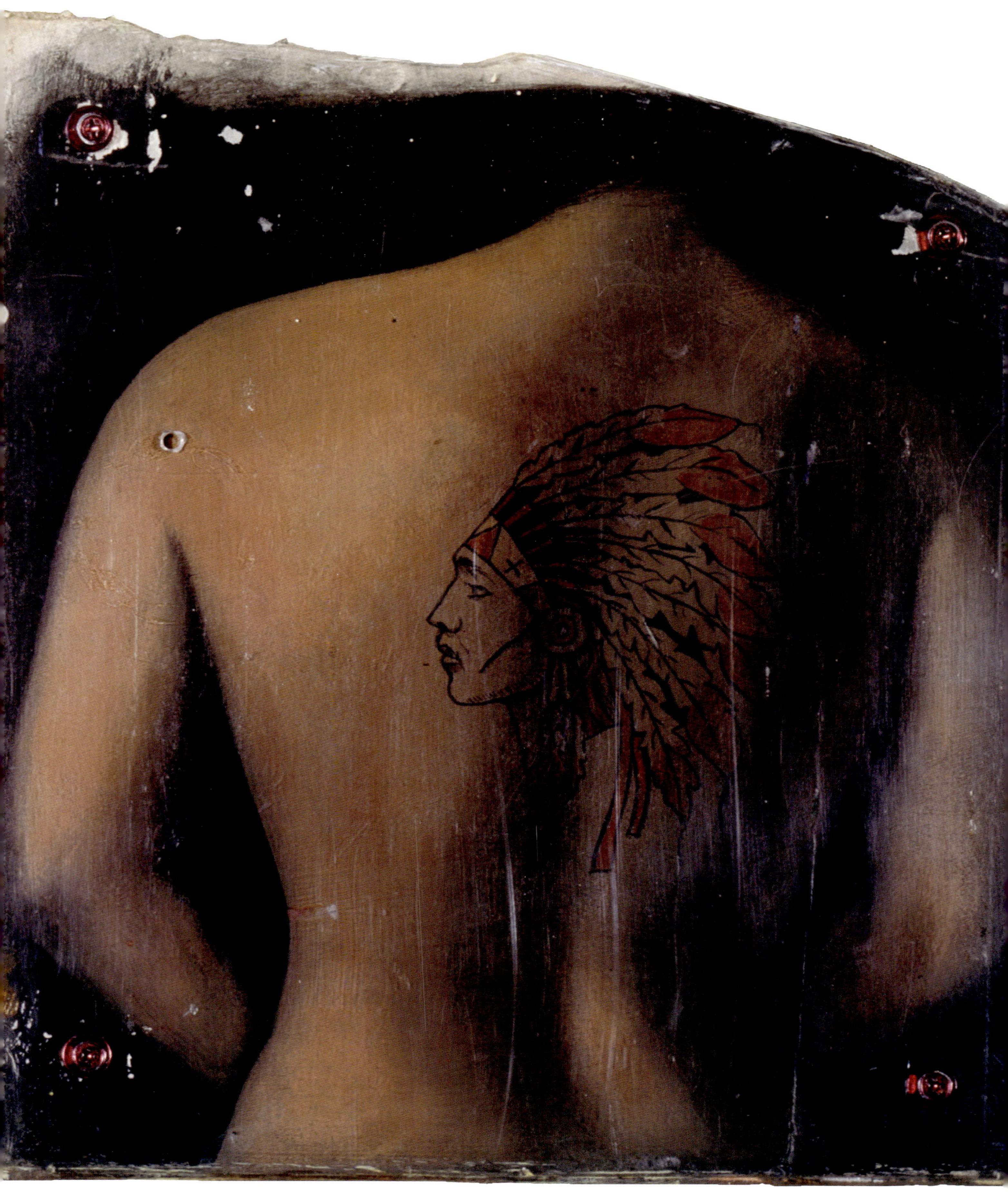

I can't remember whether it was before or after I
secretly got my first tattoo that my mother told
me about the tattoos that her father's two sisters
had. "Indian heads" she said, right in the middle
of their backs, but I don't know why. I told
this story to a Cajun man down in New Orleans
as he shared the "Rose of Sharon" tattoo planted
in the middle of his forearm. "Hmm" he said,
"sounds like a healer's mark to me". I ask
questions, but my family claims to have no
knowledge of "that sort of thing" as I
obsessively collect tattoos and any herbs, roots,
and oils I can get my hands on.

Renée Stout

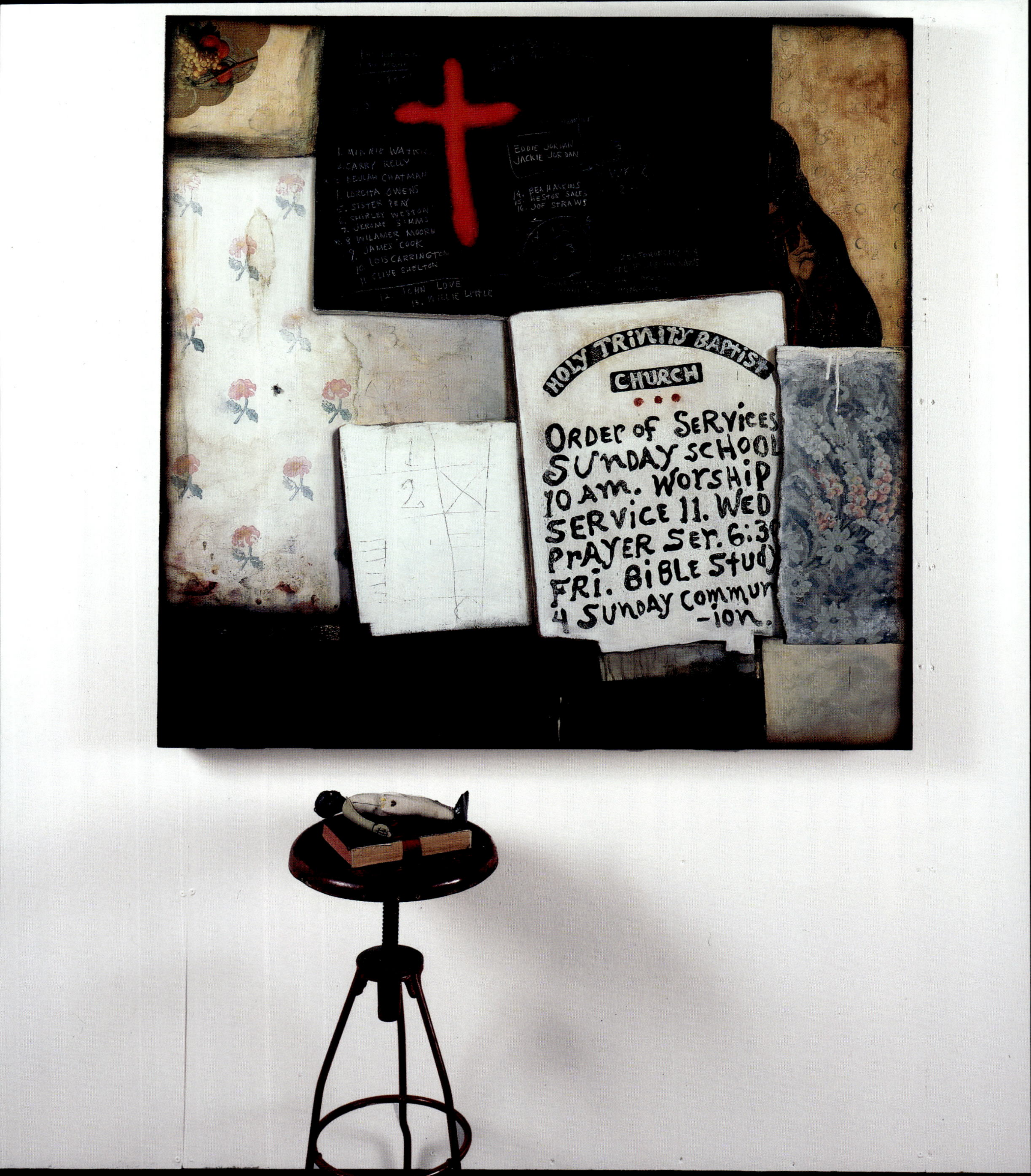

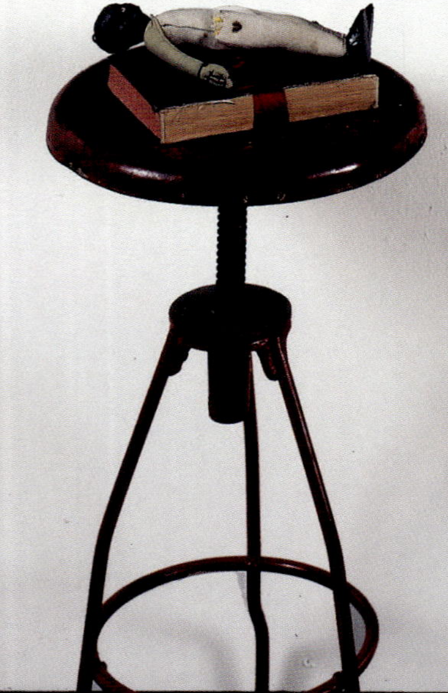

HOLY TRINITY BAPTIST
CHURCH
ORDER OF SERVICES
SUNDAY SCHOOL
10 AM. WORSHIP
SERVICE 11. WED
PRAYER SER. 6:3
FRI. BIBLE STUD
4 SUNDAY COMMUN
-ION.

Readers, Advisors, and Storefront Churches

Renée Stout

A Mid-Career Retrospective

Michelle A. Owen-Workman
Stephen Bennett Phillips

Acknowledgments

Curators Michelle A. Owen-Workman and Stephen Bennett Phillips gratefully acknowledge the tremendous effort put forth by the following institutions and individuals who have supported this project.

The University of Missouri-Kansas City
Belger Arts Center for Creative Studies

The John and Maxine Belger Family Foundation

The UMKC Art and Art History Department

The Global Arts Initiative, University of Missouri-Kansas City

Editors: Donald Garfield & Johanna Halford-MacLeod

Designer: Paul Tosh

Printer: Boelte-Hall Litho, Kansas City

Charlotte Belger, Dick Belger, John Belger, Angela Bohnenkamp, Chip Davey, Christopher Leitch, Nancy Madsen, Fred Mershimer, Jim Mobberley, Dennis Morgan, Myra Morgan, Michael Schonhoff, Alan Sells, Renée Stout, Jennifer Tanquary, and Maude Wahlman.

This catalogue is published in conjunction with *Readers, Advisors, and Storefront Churches: Works by Renée Stout* exhibition at the University of Missouri-Kansas City Belger Arts Center for Creative Studies, October 11, 2002, through December 14, 2002.

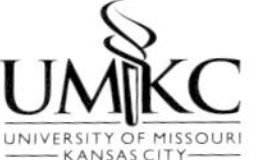

an equal opportunity institution

ISBN 0-914489-21-6

Library of Congress Control Number: 2002112456

Distributed by University of Washington Press
P.O. Box 50096
Seattle, WA 98145

Front cover:
We Do Tattoos 1999

Back cover:
Renée Stout in Her Studio 2002

Frontice piece: (detail)
We Do Tattoos 1999

Title page:
Storefront Church 2001

Page VI:
My Door 1997

Page VIII:
Packet Kongo 2000

This catalogue is dedicated to:

Ethel Beatrice Stout (1916 – 1989)

Norma Owens (born 1918)

Sara Stout (born 1938)

"Everything I am, or ever hope to be, I owe to my mother."
Abraham Lincoln

I would like to thank my family members and friends who offer ongoing moral support and encouragement in everything I do: Sara Stout, Lawrence Stout Jr., the Thomasson Family, Dean Dalton, Fred Mershimer, Dolores Dixon, Clarencetta Jelks, Anthony Awkard, Elizabeth Lyons, the Zanatta Family. I would also like to express my gratitude to Stephen Bennett Phillips and Michelle A. Owen-Workman for all their hard work and late nights, and to Elizabeth Lyons, Sam Drumgoole, Bridget Boss and all the people who participated in the workshop at More Fire. They helped me realize my vision in glass. Finally I must thank the staff of the Belger Arts Center and everyone who gives time and support to it, especially Dick Belger and Myra Morgan, without whose vision this exhibition and its wonderful catalogue would not have been possible.
Renée Stout

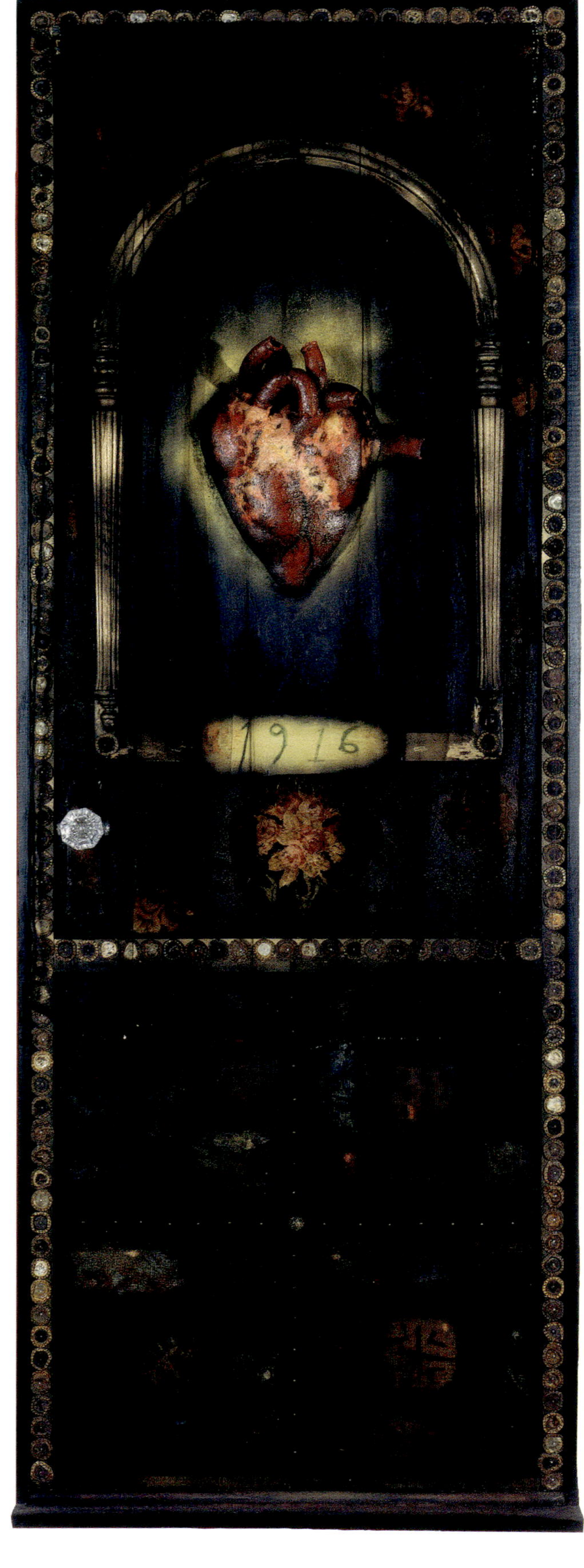
1916

Contents

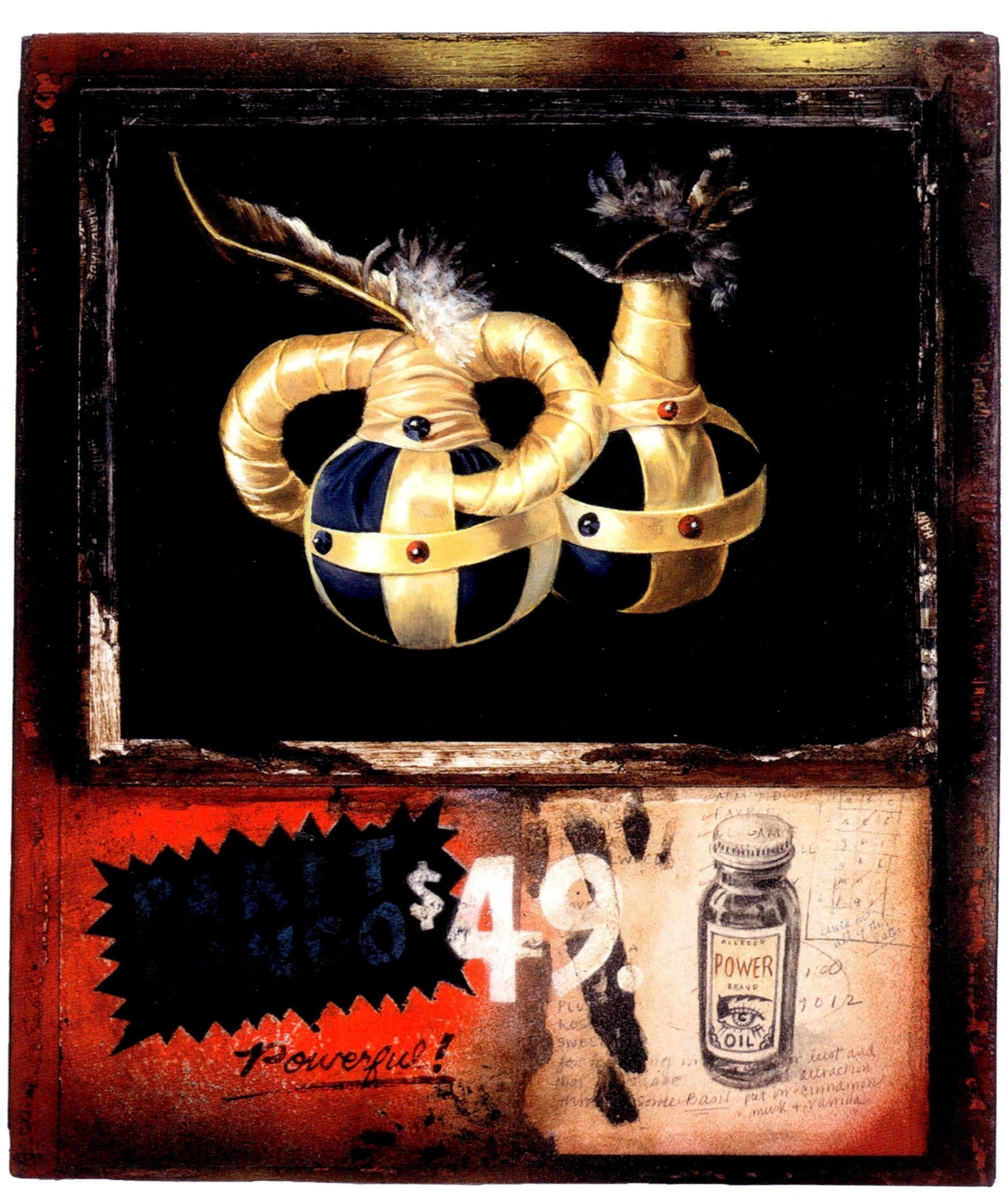
$49.
Powerful!
POWER
OIL

Foreword

Dick Belger

I first became aware of Renée Stout in 1997 while traveling to a William Christenberry exhibit opening at the Morris Museum of Art in Augusta, Georgia. Myra Morgan, now Deputy Director of the University of Missouri-Kansas City Belger Arts Center for Creative Studies, had given me a catalogue to read on the flight from Kansas City to Augusta. *Dear Robert, I'll See You at the Crossroads* featured the work of Renée Stout and was written by Marla Berns of the University of California-Santa Barbara. On my return flight, I kept thinking about the narrative sense of her work and its great personal appeal. For whatever reason, I didn't make an effort to see more of Stout's work. Two years went by before I had the good fortune to see some of her monoprints published by Joe Zanatta at the Dennis Morgan Gallery in Kansas City. I was hooked!

Some time later Stout came to Kansas City to visit Myra and other members of the Belger family and staff. To say we were impressed is an understatement. It's hard not to be moved by her treatment of emotionally charged subjects: violence, politics, economics, religion, race, sex, and gender—a volatile mix of subjects by any standard. The viewer is first drawn to the work by its muted and mysterious appeal. Only then does its full impact become apparent. Too late! Already engaged, one must now deal with it, caught in a mental version of a Venus flytrap.

Stout builds her ideas on a foundation of African-American religion, tradition, and history that reaches back hundreds of years. Certainly, African-Americans will better understand her visual vocabulary, but the universality of her images translates to non-African-Americans, as well. Somehow, the works assume an iconic nature shared by everyone, which provides a common starting point to bridge the problems of violence, politics, economics, religion, race, sex, and gender.

Although this publication is certainly not the definitive work on Renée Stout, we hope it serves to trace her career up to this point. Where she goes from here is the essence of the creative process in the journey that is life itself.

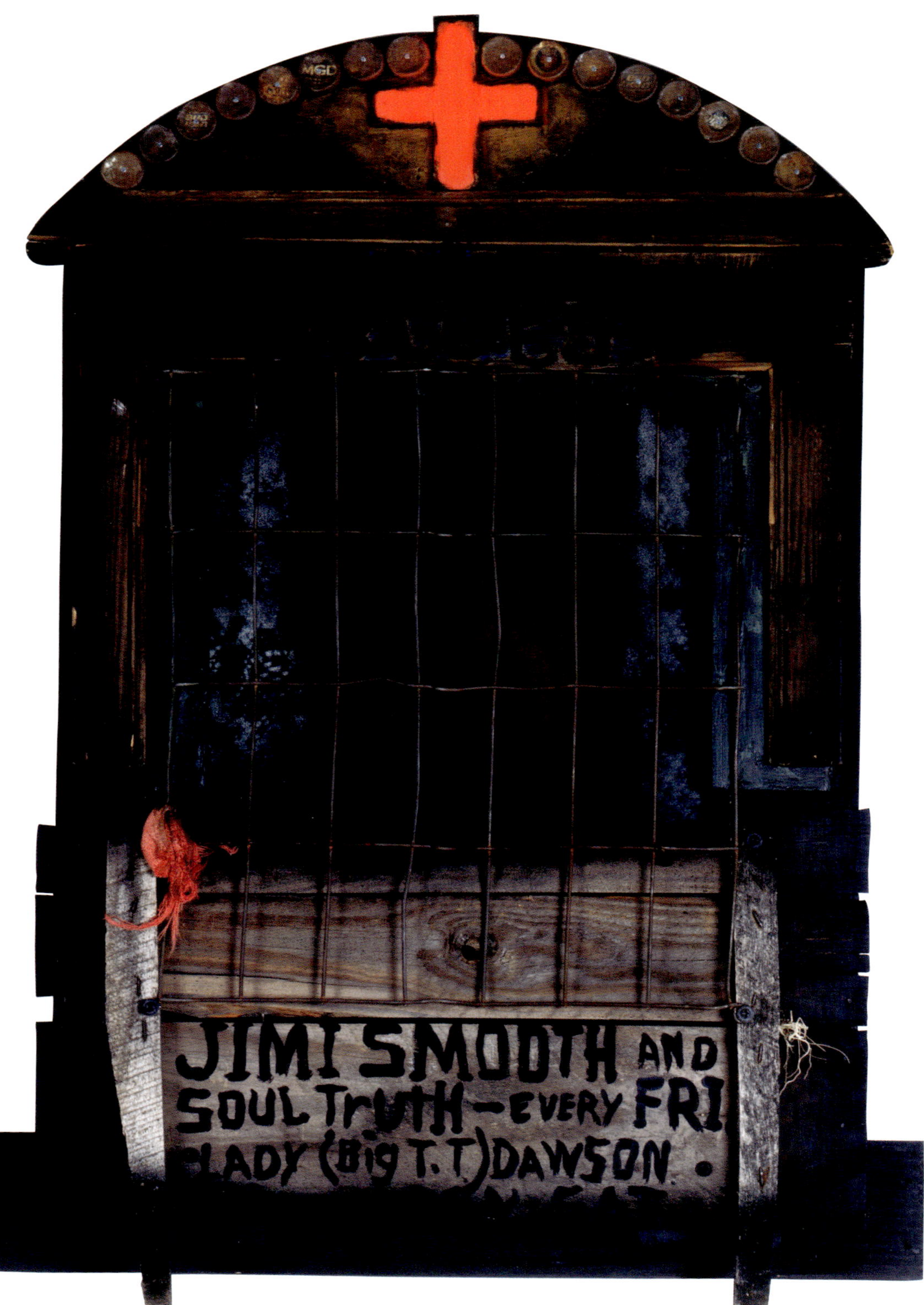
JIMI SMOOTH AND
SOUL TruTH - EVERY FRI
LADY (Big T.T) DAWSON .

Introduction

Michelle A. Owen-Workman

Readers, Advisors, and Storefront Churches explores the cultural, spiritual, and political dimensions of the mysterious world of Renée Stout. A mid-career retrospective of almost twenty years of her oeuvre, the exhibition substantially draws from the private collection of the John and Maxine Belger Family Foundation. Born in Junction City, Kansas, in 1958, she grew up in Pittsburgh, where she attended art classes at the Carnegie Museum. In addition, Stout received informal instruction from an uncle who painted on recycled materials and found objects. She earned a Bachelor of Fine Arts degree in 1980 from Carnegie-Mellon University. During her academic career, her style could be described as photo-realistic, selecting scenes derived from everyday urban life. They are nonconfrontational allusions to a peaceful, commonplace existence within the mainstream of American society.

In 1985 Stout moved to Washington, D.C., where her painting style changed dramatically. To express her burgeoning world of ideas more vividly, the artist began to experiment with mixed-media assemblages. She has said that working with found objects makes a statement about life in general. *"Use what you have and be positive, whatever it is that you have, try to make something good from it."* These mixed-media assemblages rely heavily on contemporary African-American social concerns with strong ties to her African heritage. She looks to the belief systems of various African societies and their New World descendants for direction and visual inspiration. Aspects of conjuration, root work, folklore, and music entwine to create Stout's spiritually powerful and communicative work. She summons African deities, Haitian loa, and Vodou priestesses to assist in her journey. Her art invites viewers to join her on a personal journey. Fictional narratives with imaginary characters add to the work's mysterious aura:

> *I am trying to create art that helps me put together what are only fragments, to try to create a whole, so that I can gain a better understanding of my own existence. In doing this I hope that others, no matter where they come from, will realize some answers about their own existence.*
>
> Renée Stout

Opposite page:
Juke Joint Window 1998

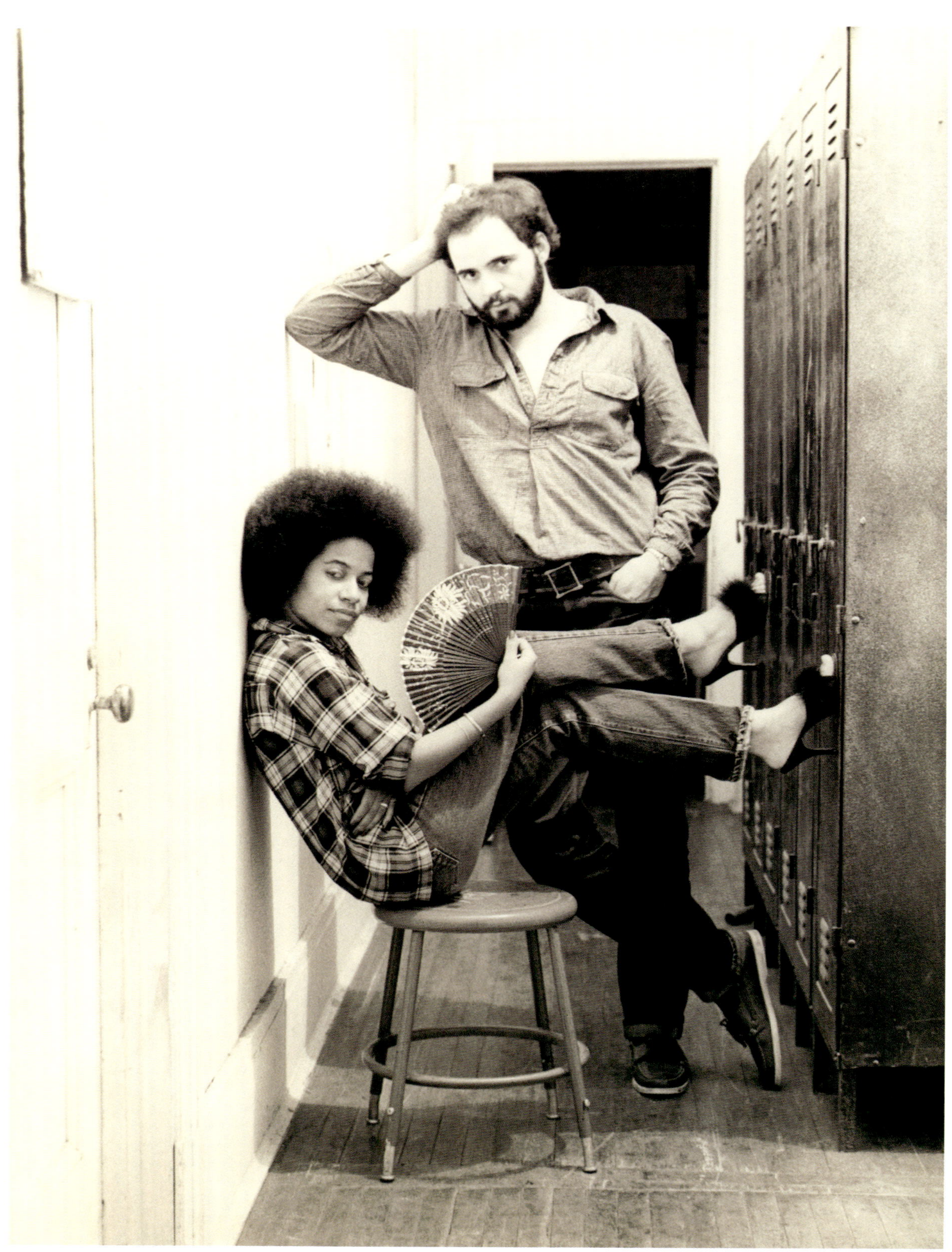

Renée Stout and classmate Frederick Mershimer during sophomore year (1977) at Carnegie-Mellon University, Pittsburgh.

The Early Life and Career of Renée Stout*

Stephen Bennett Phillips

Personal history permeates the work of Renée Stout. Born in Kansas, where her father was stationed in the Army, she along with her family soon returned to their native Pittsburgh. There, Renée and her younger sister, Lauren, spent their childhood. When he was growing up, Renée's father wanted to be an artist but family pressure led him to join the Stout's hauling business instead. A skilled craftsman able to make anything with tools, he was an important artistic influence on Renée. His collection of found objects gave her an early appreciation for the aesthetic appeal of weathered matter. Inheriting her father's creative spirit and risk-taking personality, Renée fulfilled his thwarted dreams by becoming an artist.

Stout's grandmothers also had a great influence on her early years. Both were strong women with deep religious beliefs. Her father's mother was a Baptist, while her maternal grandmother converted to Catholicism. Stout herself has never officially joined either denomination, but as a child she enjoyed going to church with her grandmothers. Stout's parents, though spiritual, were not active churchgoers, leaving her free to worship as she wished. Each Sunday during her childhood, she chose which church she wanted to attend. Mass at the Catholic Church offered visual pleasures: high vaulted ceilings, gilding, and polychrome statues of saints, animated by flickering candle light. With its full gospel choir, the delights of the Baptist church were aural. By the time she reached high-school age, Stout went to church only on occasion and stopped altogether in college, but her early exposure to different religious environments gave her a natural context for her later artistic exploration of the religious dimensions of African art.

Stout cannot remember a time when she did not draw. Her artistic endeavors began at the age of three, when she took a pen and scribbled on her Buster Brown shoes. Instead of getting mad, Mrs. Stout responded by buying art supplies so her daughter could create her masterpieces on a more acceptable surface. Mrs. Stout understood that the need to create was deep and powerful and should be encouraged. Moreover, her own brother, Jesse Owens Jr., was a self-taught artist. Since he did not have much money, he drew on anything—discarded cardboard, candy wrappers, paper scraps, etc. Sometimes his drawings were inspired by images he saw in *National Geographic* magazine, while at other times they were prompted by religious icons in his mother's house. Her uncle was the first real artist Renée knew and became an important inspiration.

**My essays were based on numerous conversations and interviews with the artist, including two extensive ones on April 27 and July 2, 2002.*

Like many mothers, Mrs. Stout covered her walls with her daughter's drawings, mostly depicting domestic interiors. Occasionally, Renée made fashion drawings and designed outfits. On canvas and with some acrylic paints her mother bought for her, she made up a scene: the silhouette of a man sitting on an island leaning up against a palm tree and thinking. It hung for many years in the dining room of her parents' home.

At school Stout was considered a budding artist. In kindergarten one of her drawings appeared on the back page of the school newspaper. In fourth grade her art teacher picked her to join an elite group of young artists drawn from Pittsburgh's elementary schools. They met at the Carnegie Museum for instruction every Saturday afternoon for three years. There, in the auditorium, Mr. Fitzpatrick lectured several hundred students for two hours about art. He was a legend in local art education circles and counted among his pupils Renée's father and his classmate, Raymond Sanders. In the second half of the class, the children visited the natural history section of the museum, where they sketched one of the objects on display for an hour. At the end of the afternoon, Fitzpatrick collected all the drawings for review. The following Saturday, he invited the students who had produced the eight best drawings to draw onstage during the lecture. He instructed them to transform their small drawings into larger works of art. Meanwhile, the other students listened to Fitzpatrick and watched their peers onstage. On several occasions, Fitzpatrick chose Stout's drawings.

Oddly, as Stout later realized, Fitzpatrick did not take his class to the see the museum's collections of painting and sculpture. For this reason, Stout's early subjects and influences stemmed from her exposure to natural history and ethnography rather than from works of fine art. One Saturday, when the line of students paused on their way through the natural history museum, Stout saw her first African object. A boy behind her shouted, "Look at that voodoo doll." She glanced over and saw an Nkisi figure, a power doll studded with protruding nails. Stout did not know what the object was, but she was fascinated by it, and from then on, she always made a point of looking at the objects in that case as she passed by. At the time, African artifacts were widely regarded simply as ethnographic objects from non-western cultures. At the Carnegie Museum they were randomly displayed in groupings on pegboard and in cases without descriptive labels. Although entranced by the African objects she saw, years passed before Stout understood their meaning.

Stout discovered works of fine art on her own. In fourth grade, she saw a reproduction of *Night Hawks* by Edward Hopper in an art history textbook. It was the first important painting to capture her imagination. What she liked about it was its realism, which she regarded at the time as one of the hallmarks of a good work of art.

But she was also attracted to something else in it that she could not describe. Years later she realized that the quality in *Night Hawks* that appealed to her was its sense of mystery and melancholy. No other work of art that she saw during grade school or high school captivated her in the same way. Stout continues to be drawn to works with similar affective qualities.

Throughout her school years, Stout had no shortage of encouragement, instruction, and supplies. Her motivation did not flag even when art classes in high school were treated as free periods. Nevertheless, she had no plans to study art in college. Science was a competing interest, having enjoyed dissecting worms and insects and examining them under a microscope. (This fascination with invertebrates is reflected in her art: insects frequently appear in her paintings.) In junior and senior high school, thinking that she might go into science or engineering, she enrolled in an academic program that encouraged African Americans to study engineering, spending her afternoons interning in the engineering department at U.S. Steel. So it came as a surprise to her parents when, on her application to Carnegie-Mellon University, Stout put down art as her proposed area of study. Her parents questioned her decision. Oddly, her father was the one who objected most strongly to her choice of concentration. As his own father had cautioned him, he told her that she might have difficulty supporting herself if she became an artist. When Renée insisted that she did not want to go into engineering, her mother sided with her, telling her husband that the decision was Renée's to make.

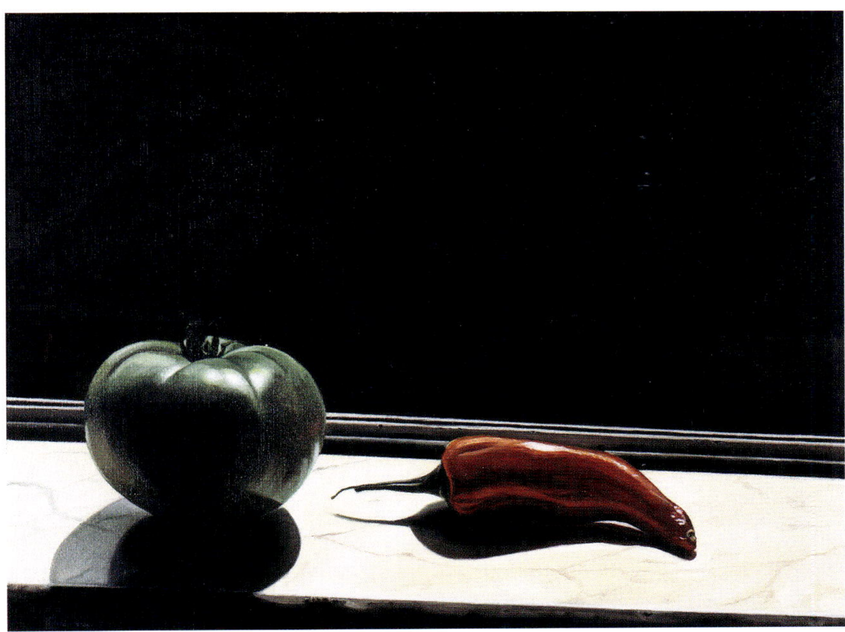

Still Life 1984

In 1976 Stout enrolled at Carnegie-Mellon University, taking a combination of studio and art history classes, as well as electives in history, writing, and sociology. She learned about her early idol, Edward Hopper, but in the classes she took there was no discussion of African art, even in relation to modern art. As Stout became more familiar with the history of western art, she gravitated towards the realist painters. This stemmed from her early love of Hopper, as well as from her childhood desire to make paintings that "looked like something." Soon she discovered the work of a group of contemporary hyperrealist painters known as photo realists, including Richard Estes and Robert Cottingham, who were popular in the late 1970s. Stout liked the way their work captured a sense of the street.

For the next ten years Stout embraced and perfected a realist style. *Still Life* shows her early appreciation of the power of objects and their narrative potential, as well as her misgivings about relationships. The composition contains just two objects—a tomato and a pepper—on a windowsill. The background glass reveals the darkness beyond the window, with only a faint reflection visible. Unlike most still life setups, the objects here are isolated from one another. In a subliminal way, Stout is making a statement about human relationships, with the robust young green tomato a surrogate for the female and the long older red pepper for the male. Stiff and distant, they stand apart from each other, like people in a marriage that has grown cold. With its sharp contrast of light and dark and its black shadows, Stout creates a mysterious context for the melancholy silence at the heart of the painting, turning her realistically rendered objects into vegetable equivalents of Hopper's lonely people.

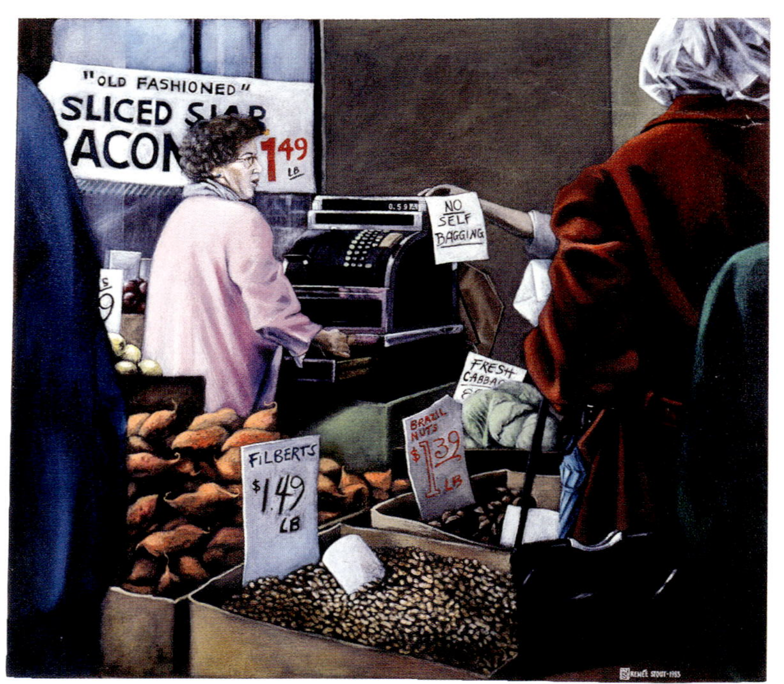

No Self-Bagging 1984

After graduating from college, Stout chose undemanding work that would allow her to preserve her creative energy and paint after hours. Working in a thrift store and still living at home, she did not have a studio, so she worked either on her mother's dining room table or in her bedroom at a drawing board and easel. When the owner of the thrift store learned that Stout could paint, he commissioned her to create new signs to hang in his store. Not confident about her sign-making skills, she decided to study with a sign painter who taught her the tricks of the trade—from

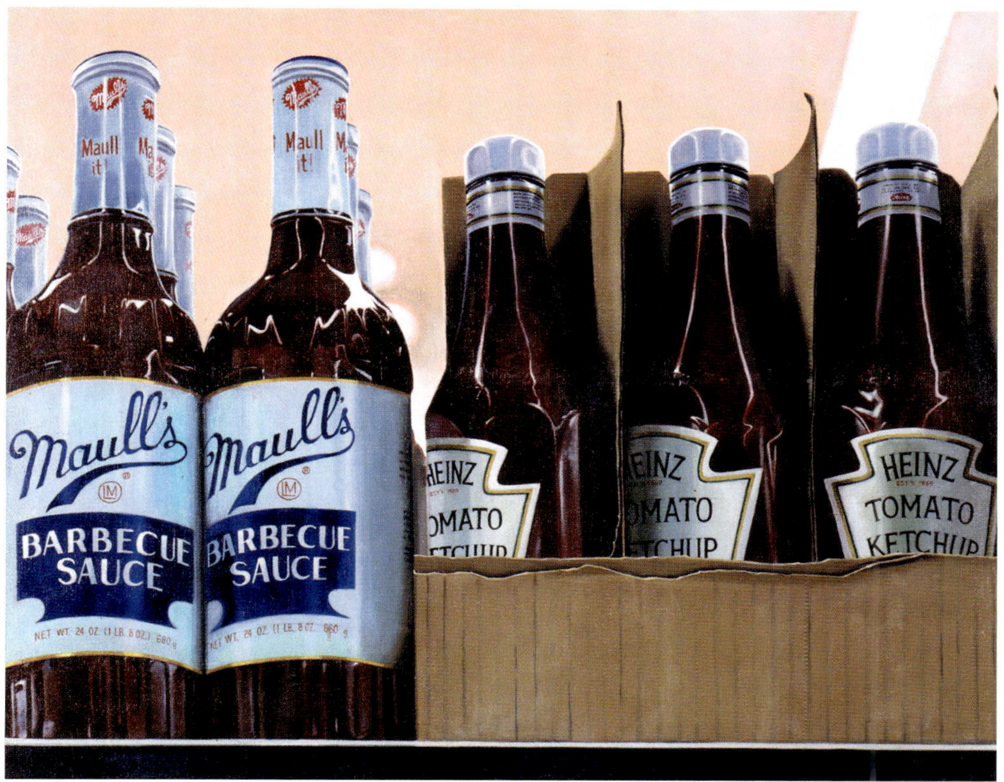

Maull It! 1985

the selection of the correct brushes for different strokes to the physical qualities of various paints. After mastering the techniques, she started painting signs and continued until she moved away from Pittsburgh. Her work today continues to show the traces of her training as a sign painter.

No Self-Bagging, another early narrative work, depicts a moment in a market. Unlike the objects in *Still Life,* which confront the viewer, the people in *No Self-Bagging* are seen from behind. The narrative focus is the cashier in pink, shown in three-quarters profile, as she finishes ringing up a sale for a customer whose hand is resting on the top of the register. Other women are lined up behind the unseen figure, waiting to check out. The painting is beautifully composed. Cropped like a photograph, the fragmentary figures on the left and right convey a sense of action and focus the viewer's gaze on the objects and drama in the center. Supermarket signs posted throughout the composition add to the work's lively realism and show the artist's continued interest in signage.

In 1984 Stout encountered the work of Betye Saar and Joseph Cornell, both artists whose careers were built on creating art from found objects. Although Stout had already incorporated three-dimensional objects in her work, she now realized that a whole work of art could be a collage of collected elements, and need have no correlative in the outside world. With this in mind, she set off in fall 1984 for a six-month residency with AAMARP (African-American Masters Artist in Residence Program) at Northeastern University in Boston. The program was started by Dana Chandler Jr., a black artist/activist, to encourage young artists. Turned off by Boston's racism, Stout stayed out of the city, stopped painting scenes of the real world, and stayed in her campus studio, dealing instead with her own psyche. Inspired by the work of Saar and Cornell, she began assembling boxes of found objects.

Returning to Pittsburgh she did some of her last hyperrealist work. *Maull It!* (Pittsburgh Still Life) is both a tour de force in the artist's oeuvre of the period and a swan song to Pittsburgh. The bottles of ketchup and barbeque sauce depicted in it are made in Pittsburgh and hold a sentimental spot in the artist's heart. In the painting, Stout uses her sign-painting expertise to skillfully recreate the shape of the bottles and their labels. Above all, she captures reflections in ways that make each of the materials represented—glass, plastic, and paper—look convincing. While the work is clearly indebted to hyperrealism, it shows that Stout is as skilled as the best of the photo realists and could have continued to work successfully in an illusionist vein. Instead, she moved on to face new stylistic challenges.

Leaving Pittsburgh in August 1985, she moved to Washington, D.C. During her first year there, she lived in several places, sometimes with studio space included. That year, inspired by visits to the National Museum of African Art, then located on Capitol Hill, she came to grips with African art. At the museum she saw, for the first time, African objects treated as works of art rather than ethnographic artifacts. Works were displayed on individual pedestals and with dramatic lighting. Gone were the faded and minimal labels of the Carnegie Museum, now replaced by descriptive texts. It was a profound experience for Stout, and each visit to the museum left her more inquisitive. She began to wonder about the ceremonies associated with each of the objects and started doing research, learning about the African diaspora. In each new environment, Africans combined their native religion with the religion of their slave masters. She became intrigued by the transformation of African religions removed from their original setting. In her studies, Stout became particularly interested in, even felt an affinity with, the Haitian religion called Vodou, because one of its elements, Catholicism, was familiar to her. One of the ways that the slaves used to hide the fact that they were holding on to their old religion was by using Roman Catholic saints to represent certain African deities. Most of all Stout found appealing the whole notion of a mixture of several religions. After all, she herself had been brought up in two radically different churches—Catholic and Baptist.

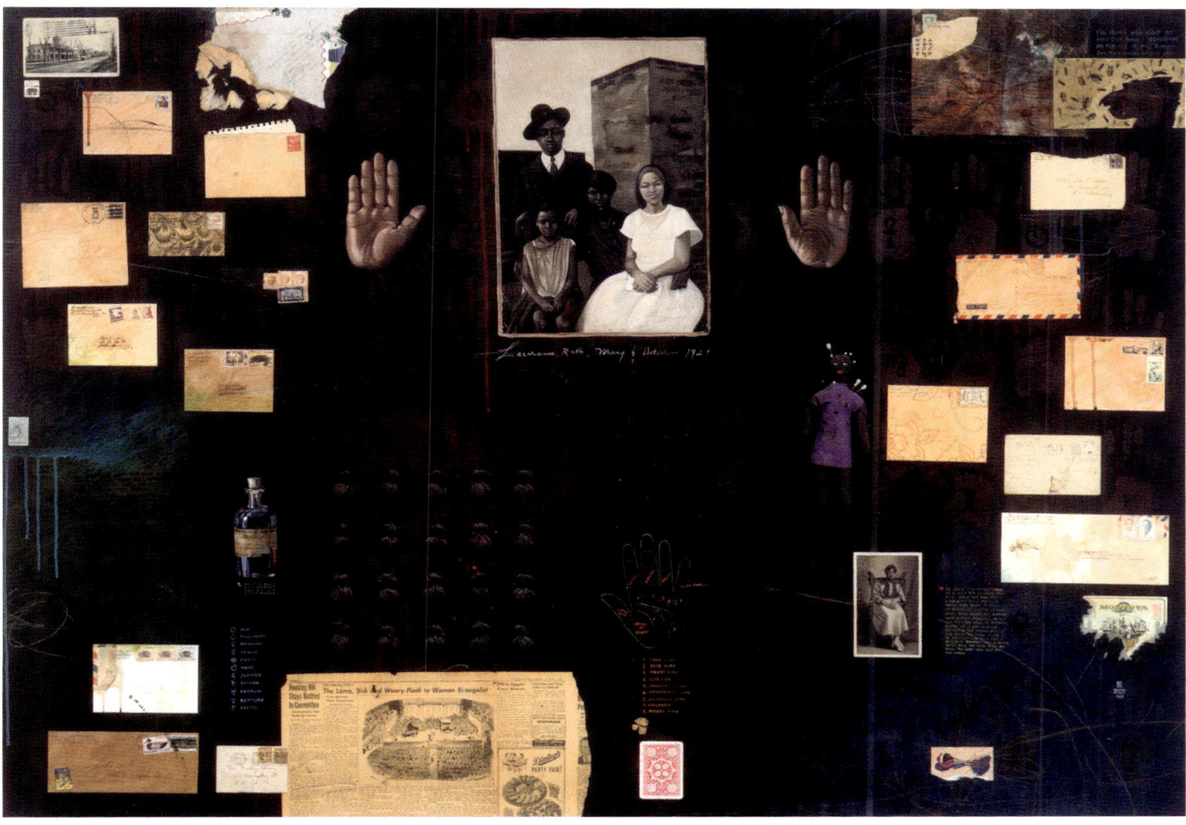

Fate Line 1987

In the course of learning about African-inspired religions, Stout became interested in root workers and fortunetellers. Reading *The Washington Post Magazine* one Sunday in 1986, she learned about an important root store in Washington and immediately paid a visit. When she walked in, she was overwhelmed. The walls were covered with layers of objects, bundles of roots and herbs, shelves crowded with jars and boxes of powders and potions, labeled and tagged, signage everywhere. She started researching the subject, discovering that many of these objects had their origins in African healing practices. Repeated visits to the store produced new finds and left their traces in her art.

Fate Line is one of the earliest paintings to combine elements of Stout's personal history with her new interest in Vodou. In the top center of the canvas, she painted a *trompe l'oeil* snapshot of her paternal grandfather with three of his relatives, which sets the tone for the piece. Real envelopes, some genuinely old and others made to look old, are placed in a very orderly fashion to left and right, giving the work a sense of personal history. In the top left corner, Stout inscribed the date 1916, her paternal grandmother's year of birth.

This is the first of many times that this date appears in Stout's work. Her grandmother passed away some time after this work was completed, and the date serves as an ongoing tribute to a woman who was so important to Stout. In the lower part of the canvas, Stout collaged a newspaper article about Sister Kathryn Kuhlman, one of several televangelists whom her maternal grandmother continues to watch. In a way that Stout now considers naïve, she introduced into the work early impressions of palm reading and voodoo culture, things that neither of her grandmothers believed in. In the center of the

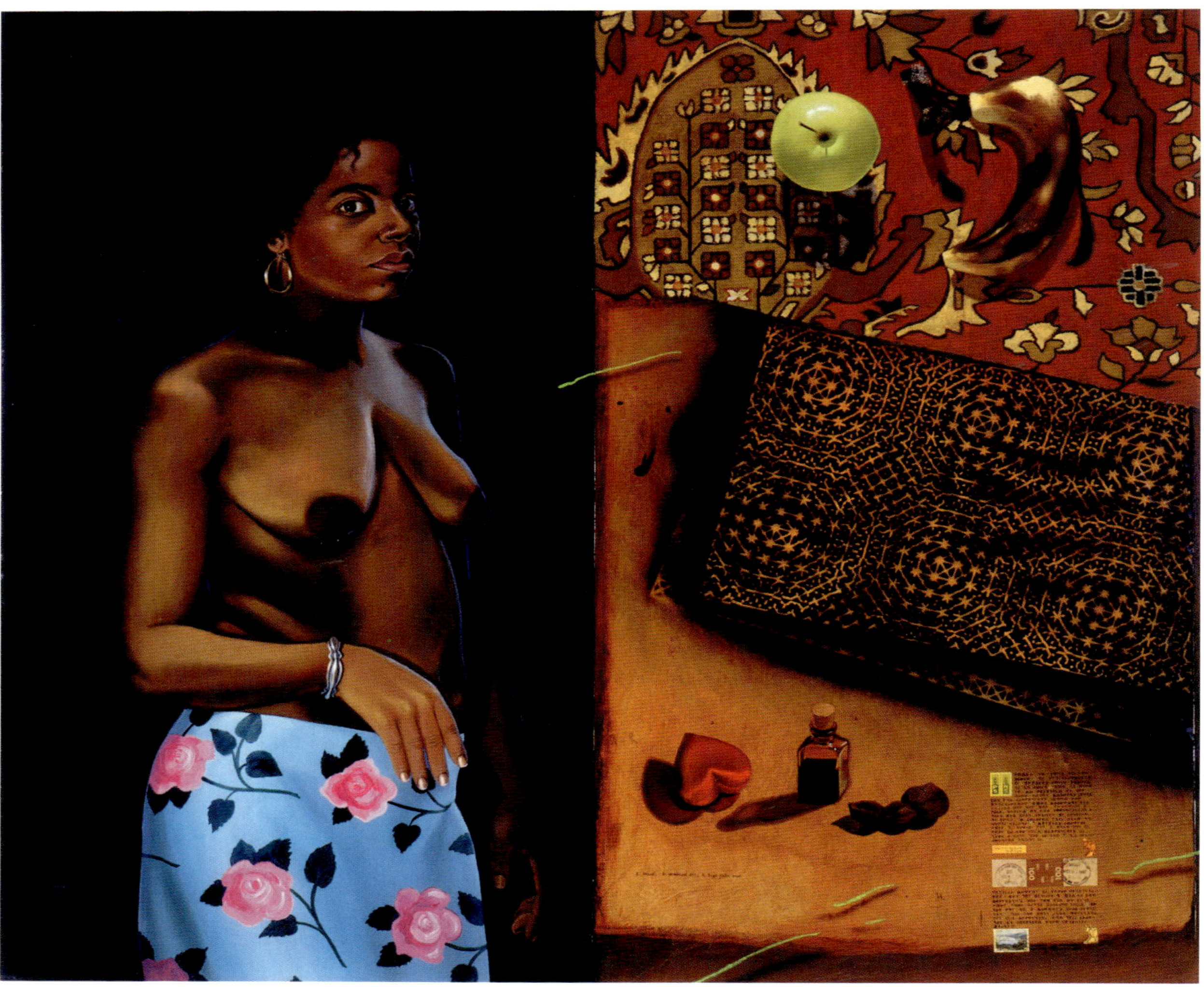

Self-Portrait 1988

canvas on either side of the painted snapshot, she includes two realistically painted hands, palms up. Visually, they dominate the composition. The palm theme is echoed in a palmistry diagram, the graphic outline of a palm with numbered zones, and in faint images of symbol-covered palms in the background. To the lower right of the snapshot is a cloth doll stuck with pins. Learning more about the subject, Stout came to regard this type of object as part of voodoo culture as seen by Hollywood. On a personal level, *Fate Line*, with its strict layout, speaks to the artist's need for order in her life at that time.

Another early work, *Self-Portrait*, was created during a summer when Stout was on break from teaching in an after-school program at a Montessori school. The picture plane is divided in half. On the left side is a beautiful self-portrait as fertility goddess, with an innocent and youthful face, full breasts, and loincloth. The right side depicts various objects as still lifes: a banana so ripe that it is past its prime serves as a contrast to the virgin goddess on the left side who is ready to bear fruit. Below the banana are root objects that show Stout's growing insight into real Vodou culture.

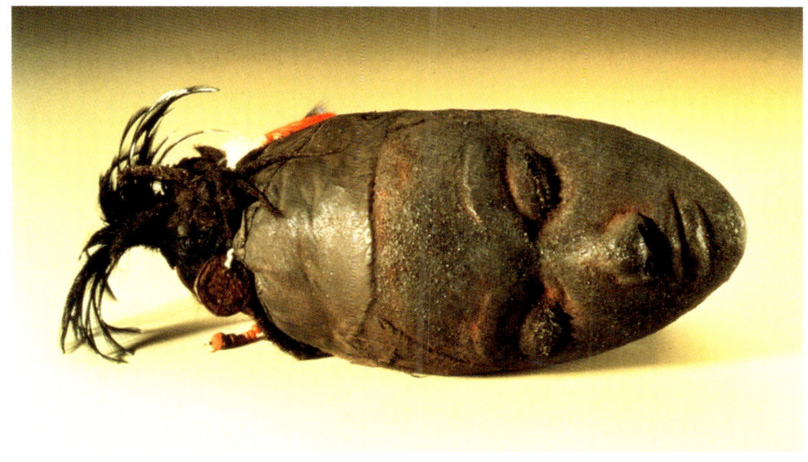

Face Pouch 1990

Face Pouch, completed two years later, shows her growing interest in creating three-dimensional works of art instead of paintings. In fabricating *Face Pouch*, the artist started by carving features into a Styrofoam wig head and covering it with layers of paint, paper, dirt, and powdered pigment. Removing the mask from the form, she attached it to pieces of leather to create a pouch. Using sweepings from her studio floor to fill the bag—sawdust, scraps of paper, and dried paint—she made an object that is essentially an art charm. After closing it with a drawstring, she attached human hair, both her own and a friend's, as well as feathers, beads, and crushed bottle caps. The resulting work rests on its side and looks like a sleeping African princess. The piece is at once a reference to African art and also an homage to Constantin Brancusi's *Sleeping Muse,* 1909-10. In a sense, Stout had come full circle by looking at a European modernist sculptor influenced by African objects. *Face Pouch* marks a new direction in the artist's work, with strong references to African art. The African quality of Stout's work can be seen in her palette of earth tones, as well as in the surface textures of rust and applied dirt. Stout especially liked rust, seen here in the weathered bottle caps. Other works from the same period incorporated found objects that had been exposed to the elements. Stout continues, in her work today, to explore the possibilities of objects' textural qualities and their capacity to express the passage of time.

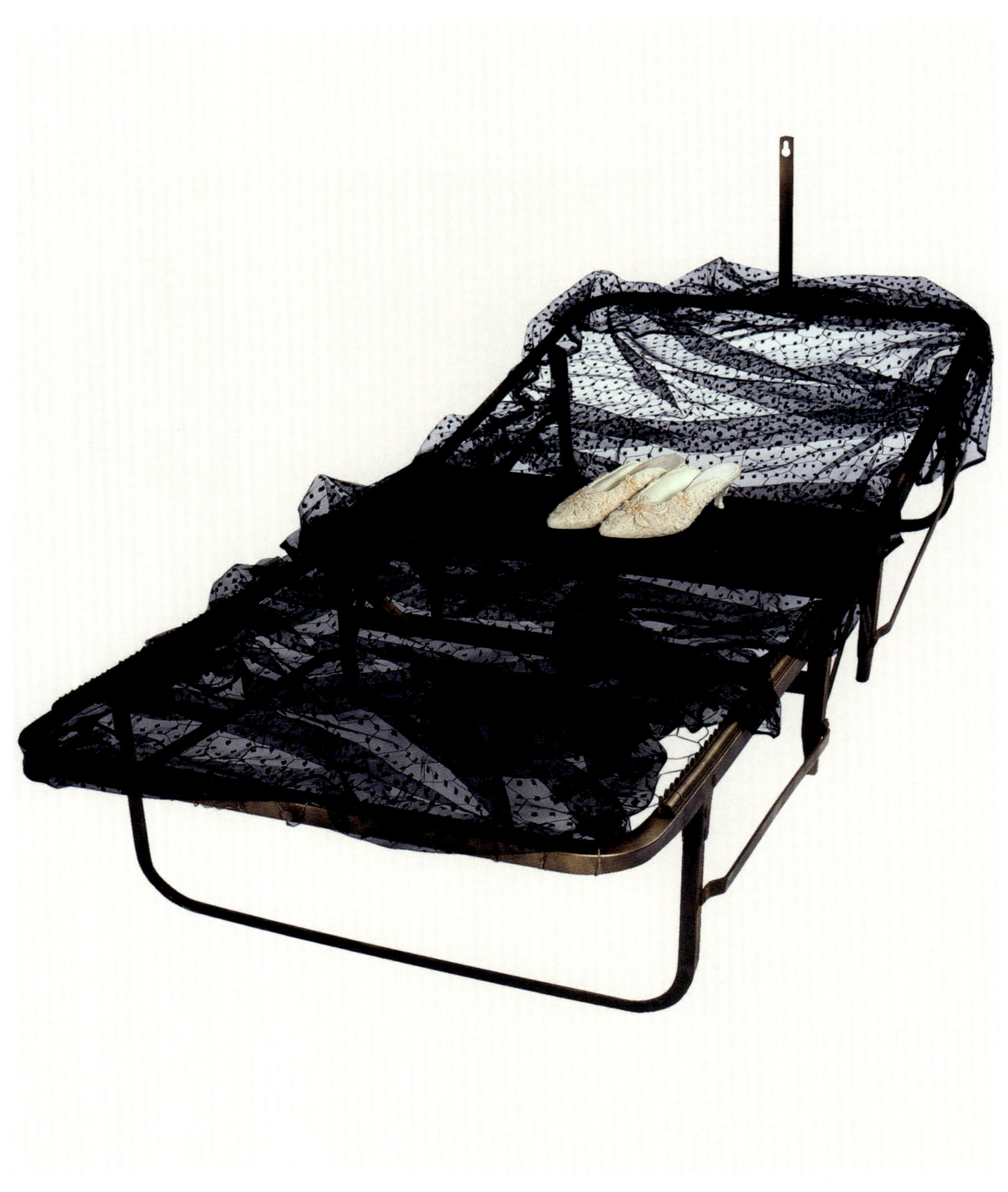

Man Trap 1994-95

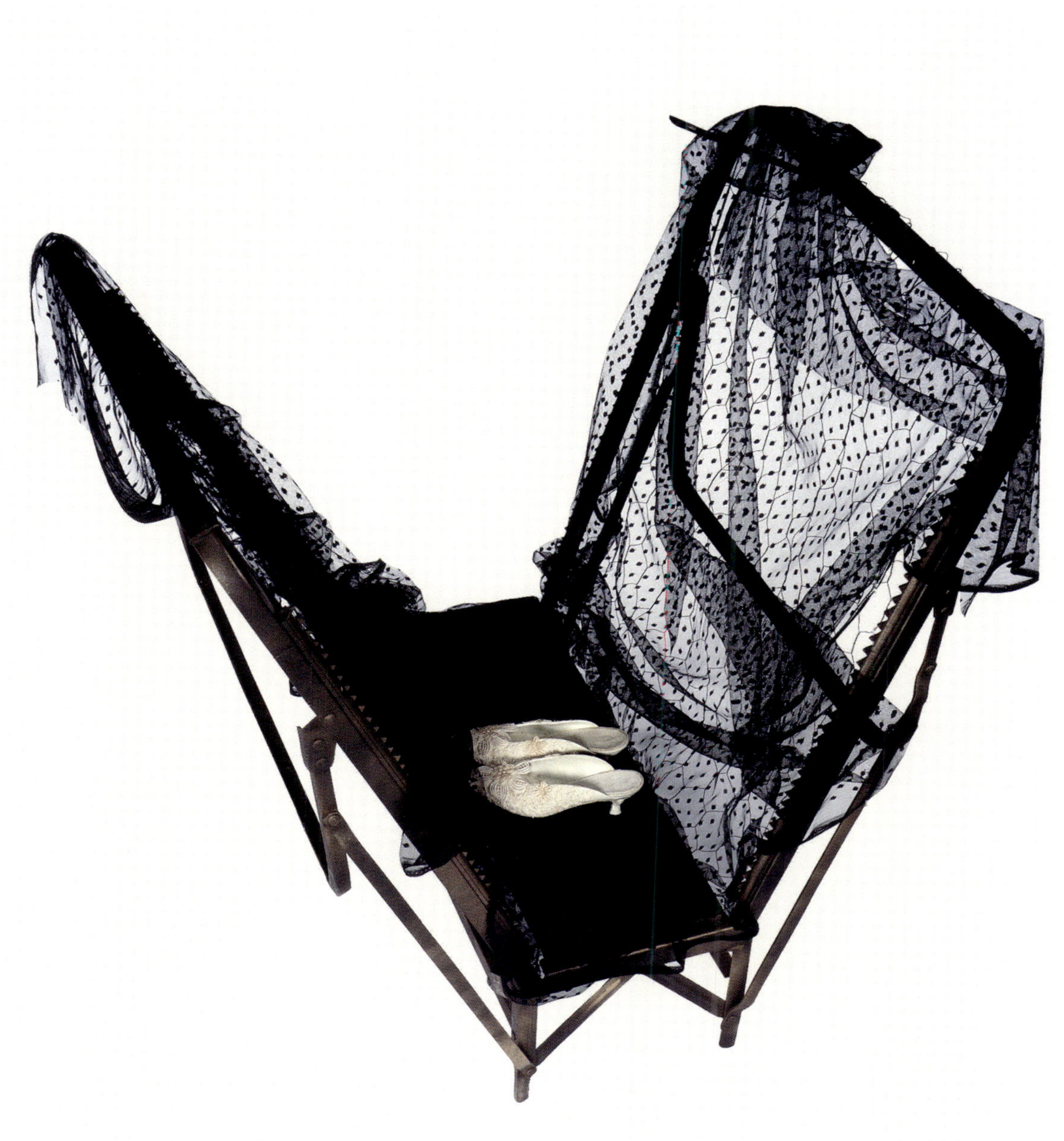

Man Trap 1994-95

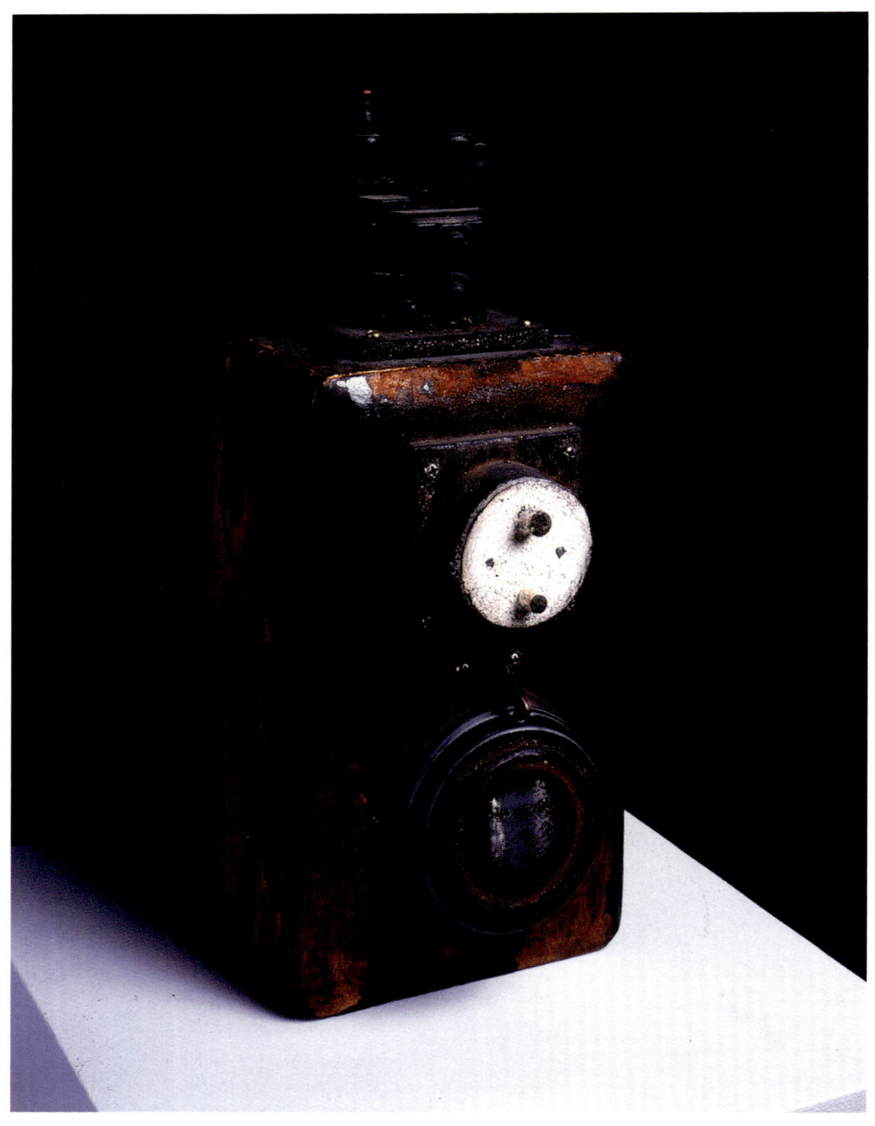

My Secrets Keep Me Going 1997

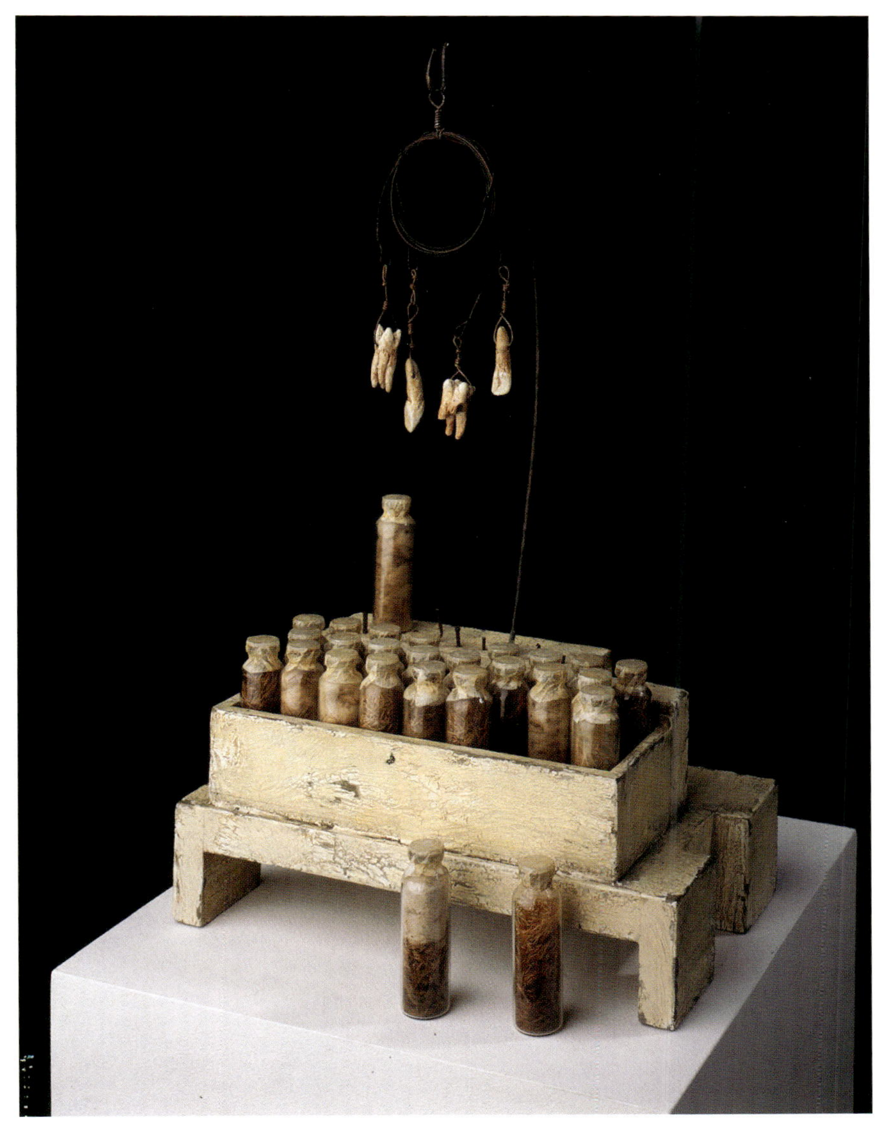

26 Whispers 1997

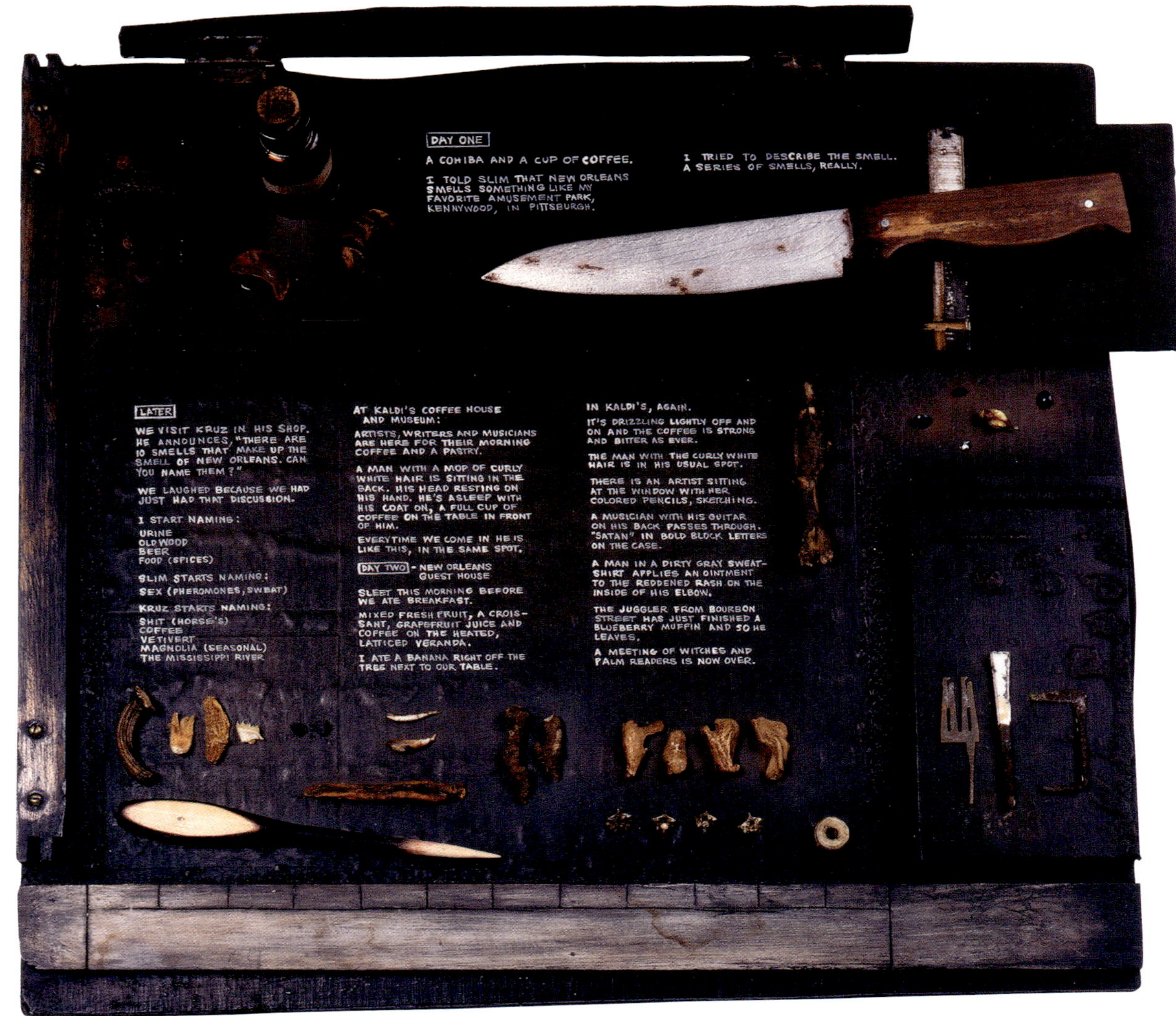

Between Midnight and Day 1998

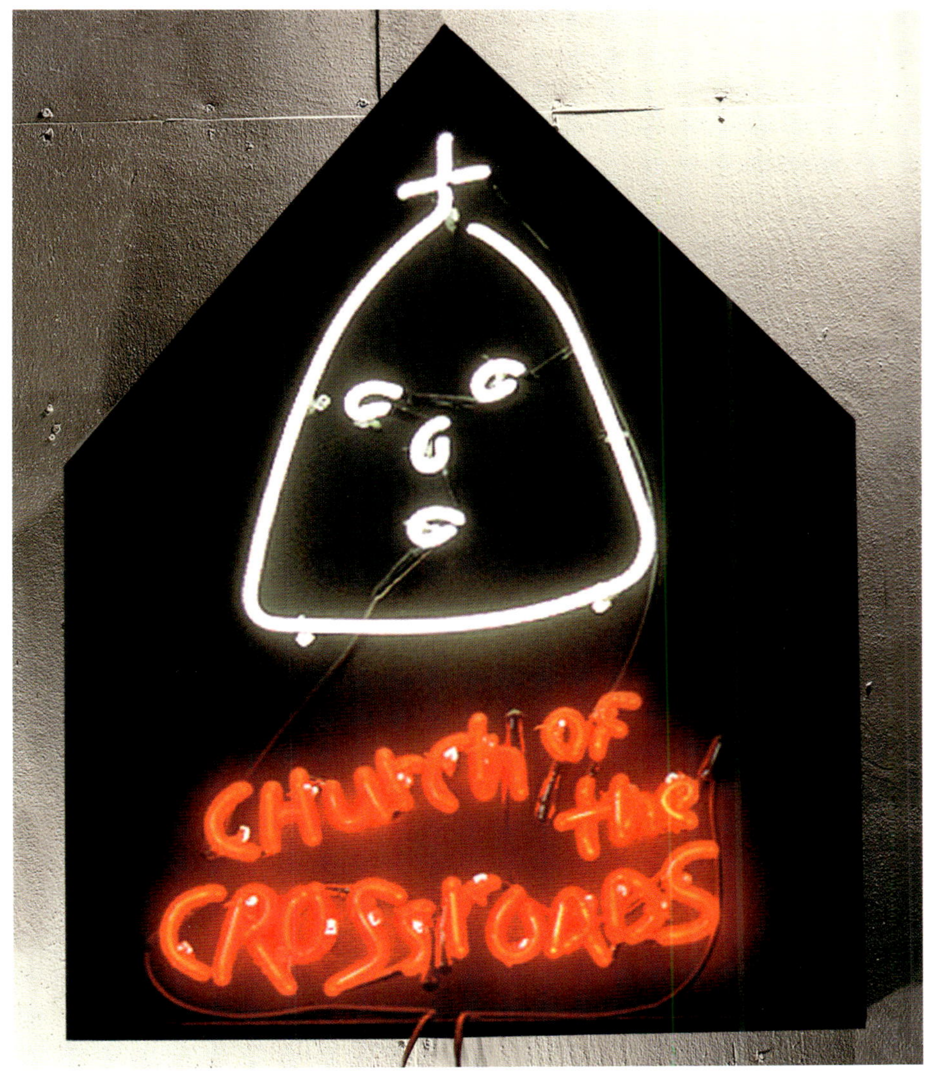

Church of the Crossroads 1999

I CAN HEAL
READINGS $2.

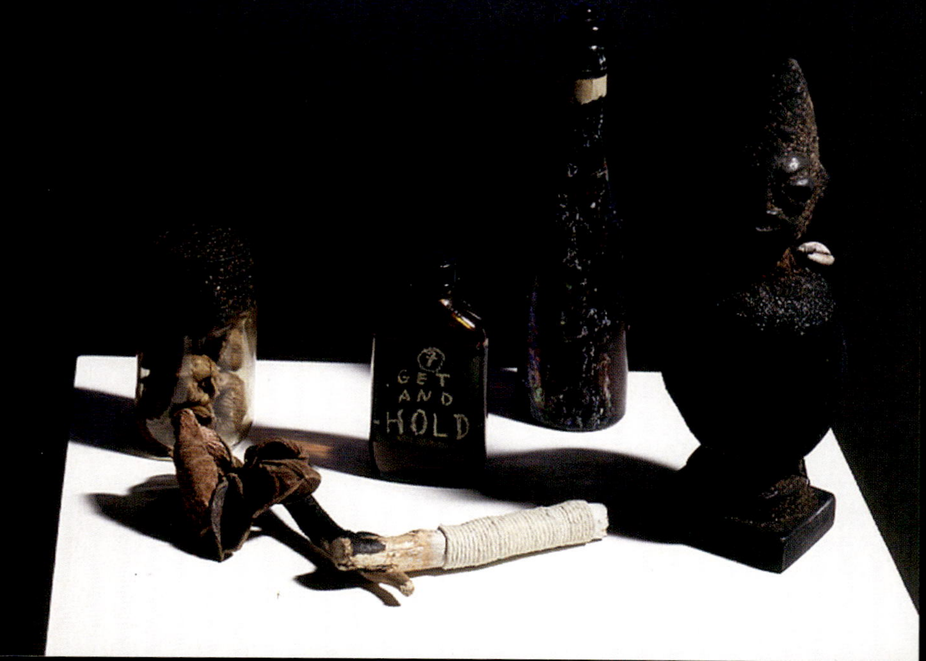
GET
AND
HOLD

A Spiritual Journey*

Michelle A. Owen-Workman

From the beginning of time, art and religion have been intertwined. Every religious tradition creates art in an effort to make contact with the eternal, making visible the invisible world of the spirit. Catholics worship God through the cross, the saints, and especially the human form of God, Jesus. Kongo priests perform divination,[1] carve *minkisi*, and assemble charms. Vodou practitioners draw *veve*, speak to the *Loa*, and create elaborate altars honoring the spirits.

Renée Stout, of African-American, Native American, and Irish descent, has always felt a kinship with societies that embrace a spiritual connection between the mortal realm and that of the ancestors. Drawing from her own background and appropriating ideas and images from other traditions, Stout has incorporated a complex combination of religious symbols into her art, almost creating a "religion" of her own. Much like Vodou, which changes according to time and place to accommodate the needs of its practitioners, the meanings of Stout's symbols are not concrete. A basic understanding of the various religious traditions that have inspired Stout, although not necessary in appreciating her artwork, deepens the viewer's experience.

Stout started her journey into the spirit world as a young child, when she was exposed to a variety of religious beliefs, both organized and unconventional. The influence of her grandmothers is reflected in the Catholic saints and Baptist churchfronts that make frequent appearances in her work. African religious elements owe their presence to Stout's encounter with an extraordinary example of a Kongo *Nkisi Nkondi*, on display at the Carnegie Museum during her childhood. Its strong spiritual presence captivated her and inspired a search to learn more about her African heritage. Another childhood influence was a house in the neighborhood that seemed to be devoted to the spirit world; Stout imagined its owner to be a spiritual healer. Later, in Washington, D.C., and New Orleans, she explored the practices of healers, but the exact meaning of the Pittsburgh house's religious imagery remains a mystery.

Much of Stout's information about her African heritage came from books, museums, and personal interpretations of objects found within her community. Even though she did not acquire an intimate knowledge

[1]Ceremonial ritual designed to communicate with the spirit world through the placement of inanimate objects. The Yoruba throw kola nuts and cast cowrie shells. The placement of the objects once they land is interpreted by a priest and considered the will of the spirits. All problems are solved through some form of divination.

**Artist references based on telephone conversations and e-mail from February until July 2002 Personal interview conducted May 4, 2002, in Washington, D.C.*

Opposite page:
I Can Heal 1999

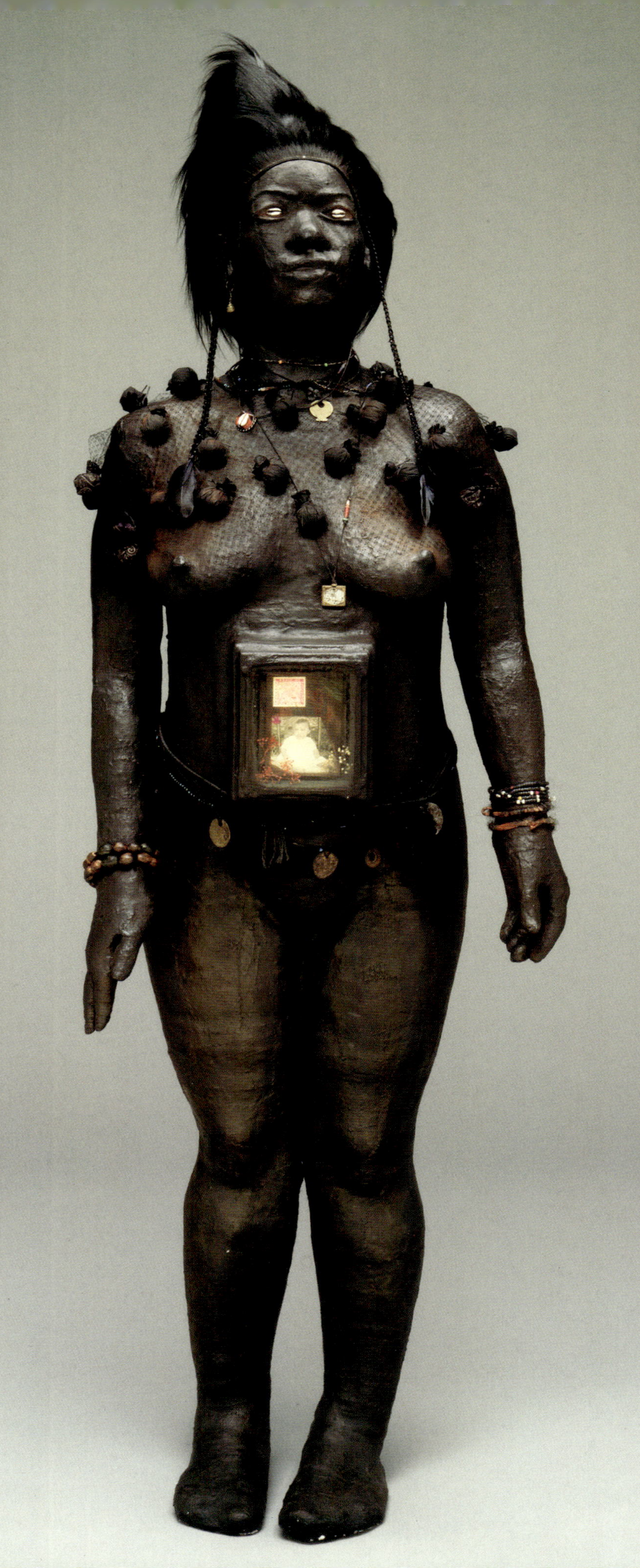

of non-European religions during her childhood, there were many examples of African-inspired objects around her. They included secret writing and hidden protective charms. Their owners often did not know the history and symbolism of these objects, but those who knew their origin could extract elements derived from African traditions. In order to better understand herself and her ancestors, Stout sought to uncover the mystery behind these objects. She began to explore beneath the surface of African-American life for its spiritual origins. As she learned more about them, Stout started to create spiritually charged images that evoke an emotional reaction from the viewer. Stout hopes that the spiritual dimension of her work will guide and empower its viewers.

In 1988 Stout created *Fetish #2*, a veritable study of her own existence. It is a modern version of a Kongo[2] Nkisi Nkondi. The life-size, nude self-portrait portrays the artist as a nkisi figure. According to MacGaffey,[3] a nkisi is a fabricated figure with a will of its own that can be invoked to produce a desired effect. It can control the behavior of people, events, and life. A Kongo Nkisi Nkondi is the largest and most powerful nkisi. In essence, this plaster self-portrait symbolized Stout's ultimate power over her own life and the path to knowledge she was seeking. Stout added various objects to the nkisi figure to give it extra power: small charms filled with medicines adorn its chest, back, and shoulders, to call upon the power of nature spirits. In lieu of eyes are cowrie shells, signifying both power and money in Africa. Dried flowers, a baby photo, and a stamp from Niger visible in the belly of the nkisi represent the power of the spirits, the innocent power of an infant, and the artist's ancestral African heritage. *Fetish #2*, one of Stout's most renowned sculptures and now regarded as the piece that jump-started her career, was first exhibited in Dallas. Focusing on its status as a female nude, critics initially failed to understand it in relationship to its African roots. The critical controversy it provoked probably helped the artist's career.

Since *Fetish #2*, most of Stout's work focuses on self-empowerment and self-healing rituals. Artworks created between 1987 and 1994 show the strong influence of African aesthetic traditions and rituals. *Untitled*, a painting completed in 1987, depicts a charm table. The ingredients used to make the red sequined bag are on the table. The conjure-woman appears to have just made a charm, using red fabric and pink ribbons symbolizing love. A miniature figure of Oshun, the Yoruba[4]

---

[2]Peoples from West Africa who greatly influenced black religions because of their numerous population in the New World. Their central belief system is based on the cosmogram.

[3]Wyatt MacGaffey, *Astonishment & Power* (Washington D.C., National Museum of African Art, 1993)

[4]Peoples from black Africa's largest population. Their territory encompasses western Nigeria and the eastern Republic of Benin. They believe in an extensive spiritual pantheon containing thousands of deities.

Opposite page:
Fetish #2 1988

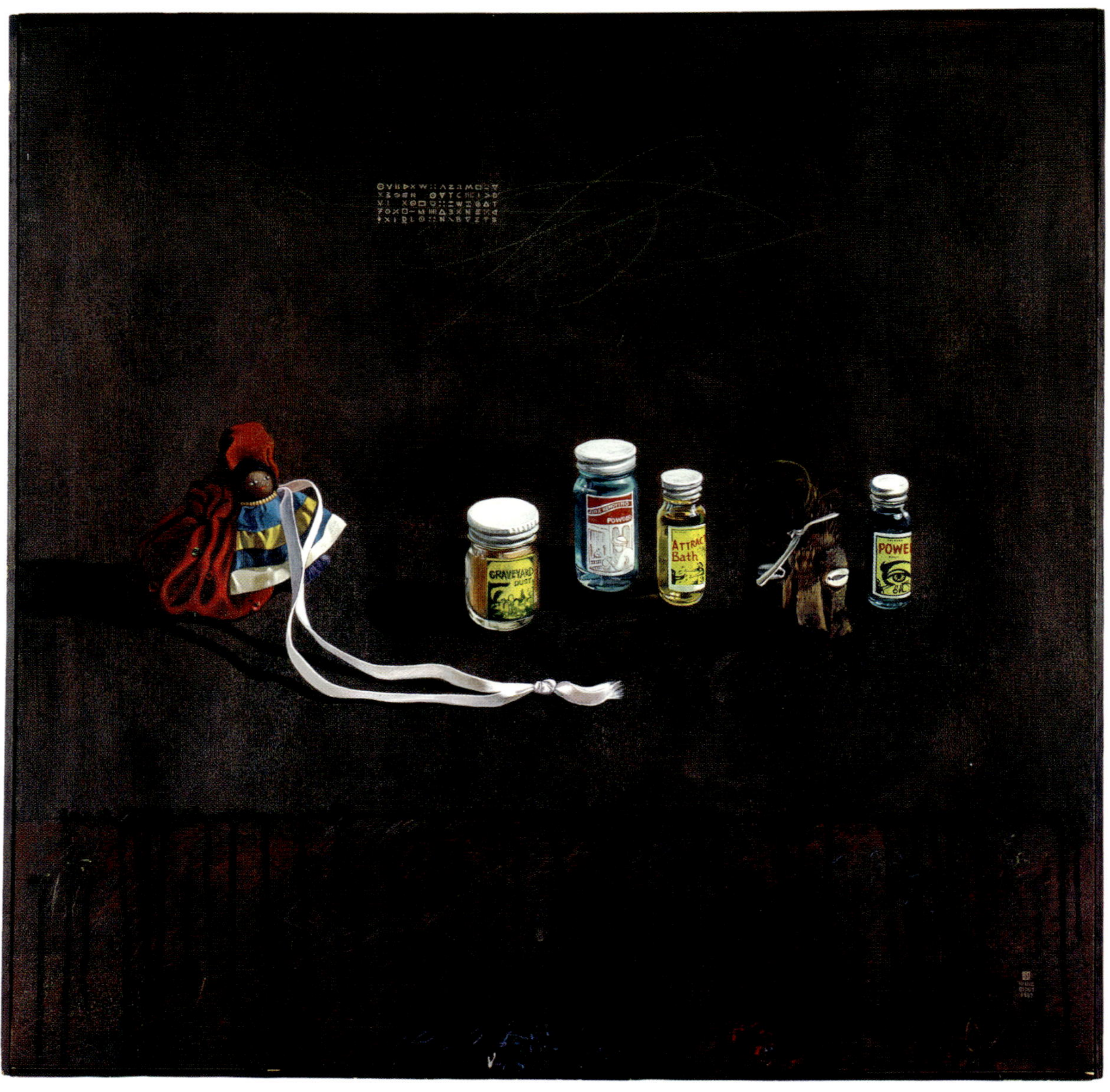

Untitled 1987

goddess of love, in her traditional blue and gold, adorns the bag. Power oil, attraction bath, graveyard dust, and jinx-removing powder are the active ingredients in the charm. A message in secret symbols painted in the background conveys spiritual powers. Although the objects depicted are actual powders and potions, the secret writing is Stout's own. Inspired by African secret writing, it is visually very distinctive. Secret societies have been a part of African social and political life for centuries. They define and protect the social roles and values of their community, communicating their beliefs through a written language of secret signs and symbols. Knowledge of their laws, symbols, and language are passed down through succeeding generations in initiation rituals, using signs that are understood only by those involved in the ceremonies. To know these ritual signs is to have power over nonmembers. Through secret writing or indecipherable script, spirits communicate with priests, who receive the secret scripts while possessed by spirits. When the priest is released from this state, the meaning of the writing becomes a mystery, even to the priest himself.

Around 1993-94 Stout became interested in the rituals and traditions that found their way to the New World from Africa. West African inspired images remain an important part of her work, and allusions to West African religions are a base onto which Stout layers references to other religious beliefs and practices. At times, it is difficult to separate the individual elements and determine their place of origin. Several of her pieces are reminiscent of Vodou rituals performed in Haiti and New Orleans and include representations of Haitian Loa.[5] Numerous West African slaves were transported to the French colony of Haiti. They created the framework for what is now the Vodou religion, combining West African religions including Vodou with the Roman Catholicism of their French masters. One example is the Catholic candle being placed in the center of a veve[6] drawing. Africans and their descendants commonly practice more than one religion. Haitians embrace this duality and believe it strengthens their religious convictions. They view this behavior as a spiritual insurance policy rather than hypocrisy. Yet, Vodou claims there is only one God, Bondye. There are three additional orders of spiritual beings: the Loa, the twins, and the dead. Loa are the various spirits of family members and the spirits of the major forces in the universe; for example, good, evil, and health. Virtually all Vodou spirits, or Loa, are associated with specific Catholic saints. For example, Erzulie,[7] the goddess of love, is paired with the Virgin Mary and Dumballah[8] is coupled with Saint Patrick. The twins represent contradictory forces in the world such as good and evil, happy and sad, male and female. Finally, the dead consist mainly of the souls of one's own family members who have died but have not yet been "reclaimed" or honored by the family. Ignored, these deceased family members can become dangerous to the living. Vodou priests, or *houngans*, devote their lives to communication with the spirits. They are mediators between the two worlds.

The most important aspect of Vodou is healing people from physical and mental illness. Vodou priests have a long history of making crude but sometimes effective herbal remedies. Various herbs and roots are

---

[5]Spirits in the Haitian Vodou pantheon. Each serves various functions in the universe. Examples are Loa of agriculture and Loa of death. Loa also can be the spirits of dead family members and related symbols.

[6]Vodou ceremonial drawings done in flour or cornmeal on the ground. Veve symbolically depicts the various Loa before a ceremony and is derived from African writing traditions.

[7]Loa of love and lust represented by a heart. Derived from the Yoruba goddess Oshun.

[8]Loa who is the master of all waters. His symbol is the snake.

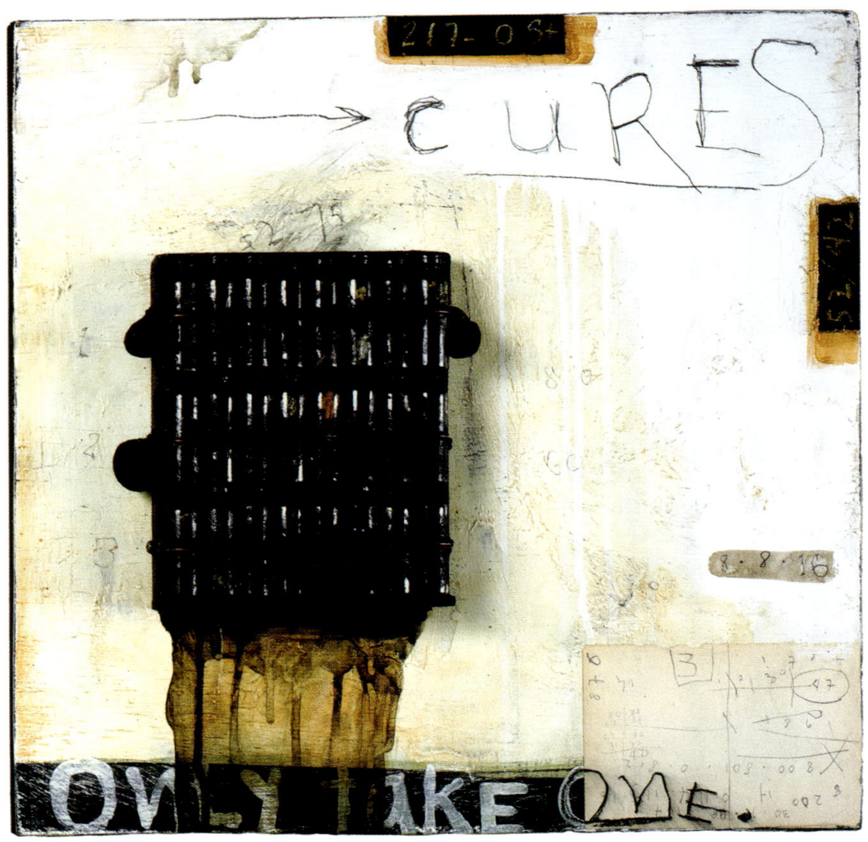

Cures 2000

boiled to create a tea or the ingredients are combined and placed in a protective casing, which is worn by the patron. Healing society's ills is a significant theme in Stout's work. In *Cures,* constructed in 2000, Stout placed glass bottles on a sign that reads, "Only take one." She is offering viewers a solution to their problems and giving them the freedom to choose which herbal remedy they deem appropriate. Twenty-four bottles tied with copper wire offer a choice of potion. Each bottle contains different objects: scraps of paper, wood, dirt, and plant material, all items either connected with nature or communication. The exact identity of the contents is obscured by sawdust and resin that cling to the surface of the glass. Another work about healing combines religious traditions. *Hoodoo Holy* depicts a bottle used in the Catholic Church for holy water with written text outlining a recipe for a Vodou potion in the upper left hand corner. Unbeknown to the casual viewer, the bottle actually contains special aromatic oils. Within one simple image, Stout has created an icon that simultaneously denotes healing, the washing away of sins, and renewal.

In Vodou, fatalism is overwhelming. During life on earth, all aspects of existence are determined by the Loa. To change anything in one's life, from a grave illness to the current political system, one must ask the Loa for help. Vodou priests conjure the spiritual power of various Loa to alleviate pain and resolve disputes. To conjure the spirit of the Loa, they conduct a ritual that incorporates drums, dancing, and possession.[9] The opening of the ceremony is marked by the priest taking water and lifting it in the direction of the four points of the compass, thereby creating the symbol of a cross or X. This central image in Vodou is defined as the crossroads, the point where the worlds of earth and spirit meet. One crossroad symbol originated in Congo as the cosmogram, denoting the four realms of the universe and the continuity of human life. It reads counterclockwise with the eastern point symbolizing birth, the north life, then death, and the southern point rebirth. Virtually all Vodou acts, even healing, begin with the acknowledgment of the crossroads. This action summons the Loa and invites them to participate in the ceremony. A candle is then lit and the first veve is drawn with cornmeal or flour. The first figure drawn is a circle. If a specific Loa is needed for the ceremony, his or her symbol is drawn: for example, a heart for Erzulie or a cross for Legba.[10] The veve may be very elaborate or simple geometric forms. During the ceremony, food offerings and sacrificed animals are placed on top of the veve. Vodou practitioners believe that animal sacrifice releases life.[11] Therefore, in some instances, bones are a metaphor for life and nature, not death.

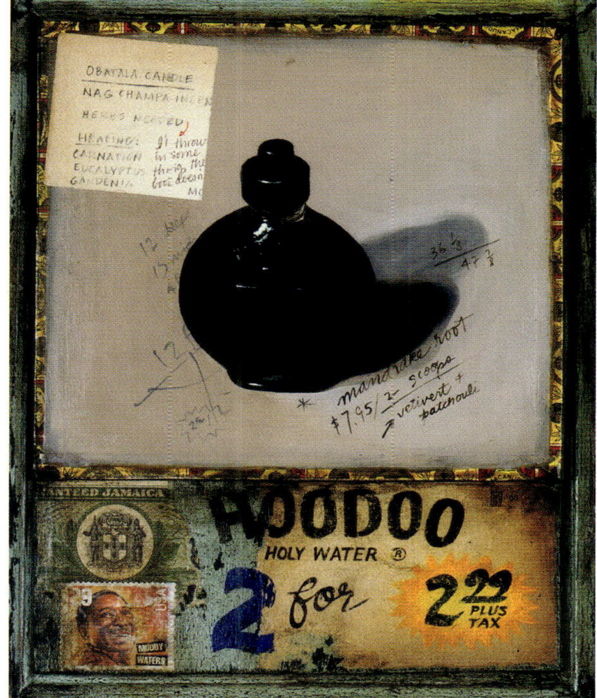

Hoodoo Holy 2000

Numerology is a pervasive element in Stout's work. In the Vodou religion, combinations of numbers symbolize various deities and concepts. As with other iconographic elements in Stout's work, the numbers function on many different levels. The number three, Stout's favorite number, signifies the presence of Legba. Erzulie's number is five, the number of love. Ogún's presence is denoted by the number four or any combination of digits adding up to four. Stout's choice of numbers is also based on personal preference. For example, she dislikes the number eight and rarely uses it in her work. Seventeen is taboo because it equals eight. Some of the numbers she uses refer to the birth year of a close relative. Stout often places her birth year, fifty-eight, near 1916, that of her paternal grandmother. When the numbers are written

[9]Loa often come to a ceremony or ritual and possess the priest or priestess. Vodou theology says the Loa take over the individual's body during possession and release it afterwards. The individual will not remember events that occurred during possession.

[10]Yoruba guardian of the crossroads. Messenger between mortals and the spirit world.

[11]Maya Deren, *Divine Horsemen* (New York, McPherson & Company, 1953)

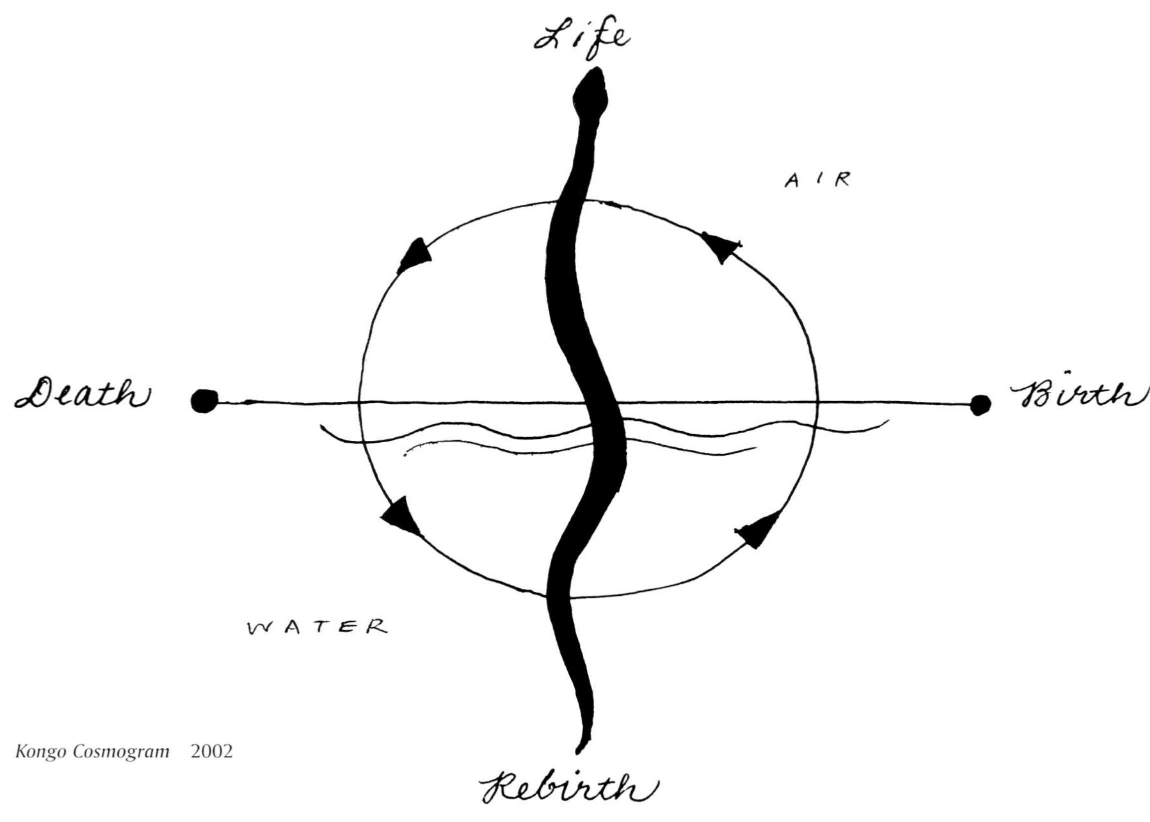

Kongo Cosmogram 2002

sequentially, they refer to the organization of daily events. When Stout turned forty, counting became a metaphor for the passing of time. Numbers can be a focal point, form the background of a piece, or take a more ancillary, but ever present role.

Stout's *Legba's Lesson Learned* incorporates an overwhelming combination of references to Legba, the Yoruba god of unpredictability. A cross with the Kongo cosmogram pointing to the four cardinal directions is positioned in the upper left hand corner. A dark figure with cowrie shell eyes, nose, and mouth comes out of the shadows above another Kongo cosmogram. Legba's signature colors—red, black, and white—work in contrast to depict the images in a dramatic composition. The number three signifies the presence of Legba. It can be denoted as the numeral three within a circle and square or by the use of numbers that add up to three. Thus, Legba can be denoted by twenty-one or twelve, because the digits in each case add up to the number three. All three possibilities are represented in *Legba's Lesson Learned*.

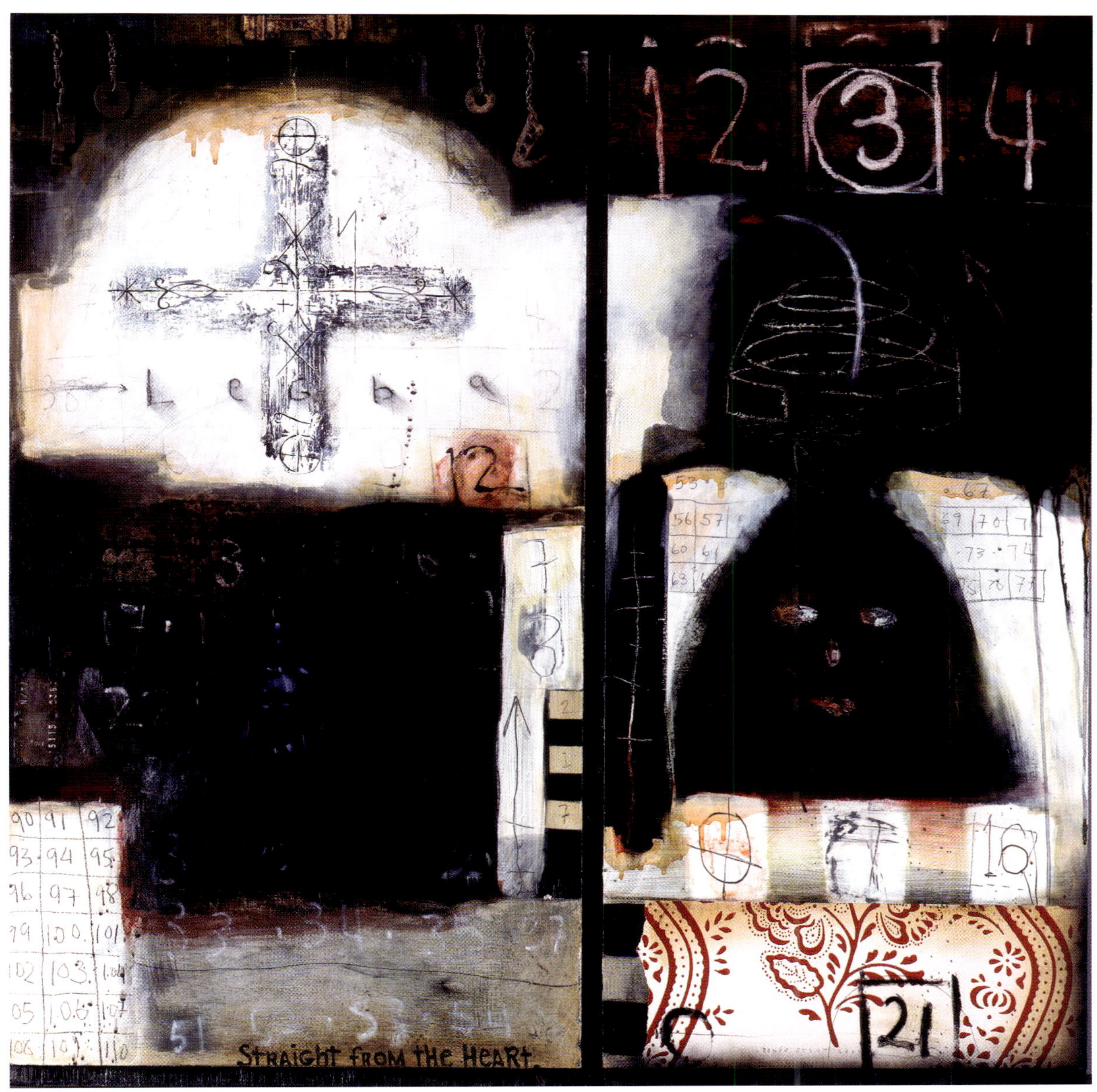

Legba's Lesson Learned 2000

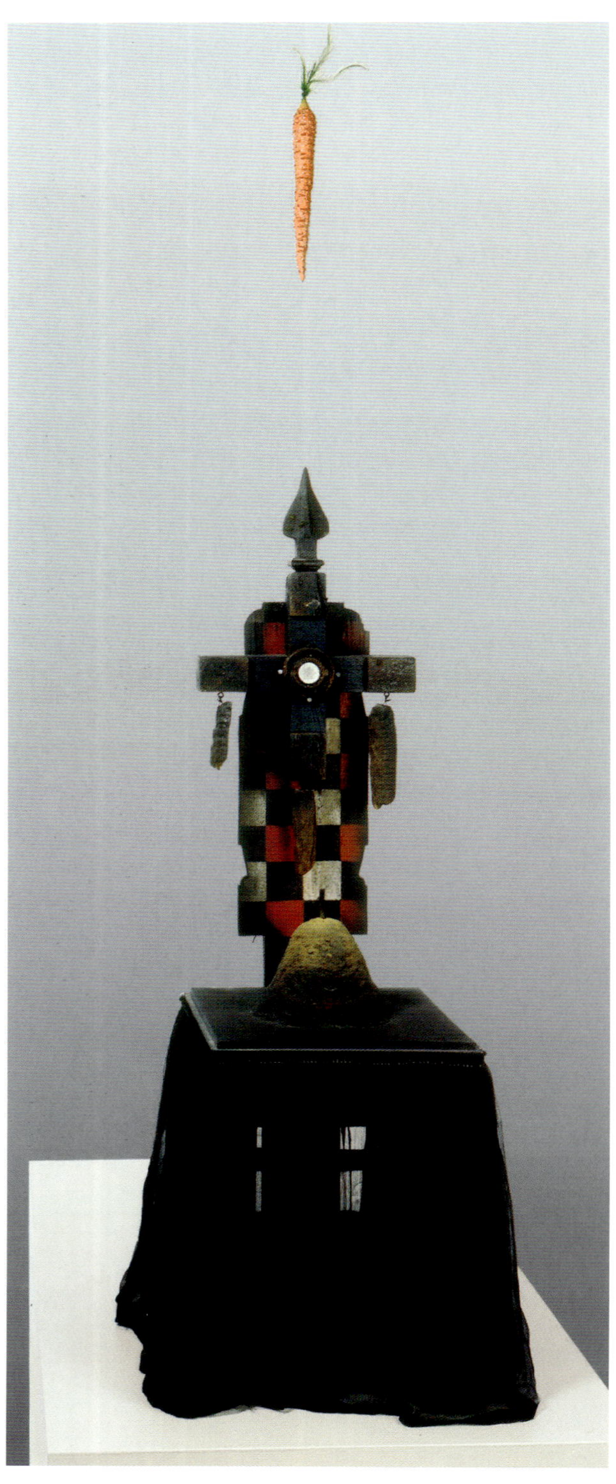

When It Comes to Love, Elegba the Trickster Dangles a Carrot in Front of My Face 1994

When It Comes to Love, Elegba the Trickster Dangles a Carrot in Front of My Face is the physical embodiment of the crossroads. Legba, also know as Eshu, is the Yoruba guardian of the crossroads. In West Africa, he is depicted as a conical pillar of red dirt, often with a sharp object protruding from the apex. Stout has placed the mound of dirt on top of a European style chair, which is reserved for royalty and spirits. The form of a cross adorns the back of the chair with a mirror in the center to deflect the power of evil spirits. Red, black, and white checkered squares, Legba's preferred colors, ensure the spirit's complete attention. The dangling carrot adds a modern metaphorical twist to the piece, disclosing the trickster aspect of Legba and his relationship to Stout. "[Legba] can never quite give me what I want or need, just sort of holds it up there for me to see, but keeps it out of my reach."[12]

Stout draws inspiration from a traditional Vodou ritual ceremony in *At the Gate of Kalfou*. The work is a sort of invocation of Kalfou and Baron Samedi to guide the spirit of Larry (Brock) Morgan, a young African-American boy who lived in Stout's neighborhood and whose murder inspired Stout to create the piece. Kalfou is considered to be the spirit of the night and the origin of darkness. He controls the evil force of the spirit world and the in-between points of the crossroads. He allows for the onslaught of bad luck, deliberate destruction, misfortune, and injustice. Kalfou symbolizes Morgan's tragic death. Baron Samedi is the Haitian Loa of death and resurrection, depicted as a black man wearing a top hat and long coat. Baron Samedi welcomes Morgan into the afterworld saying, "Come on in Brock and don't even worry about it. We walked through hell and turned it into the blues." The peppermint candy and Tabasco sauce may be food offerings to the Loa, while the lock and key may symbolize

[12]Marla C. Berns, *Dear Robert, I'll See You at the Crossroads* (Santa Barbara, The Regents of the University of California University Art Museum, 1995) p. 24.

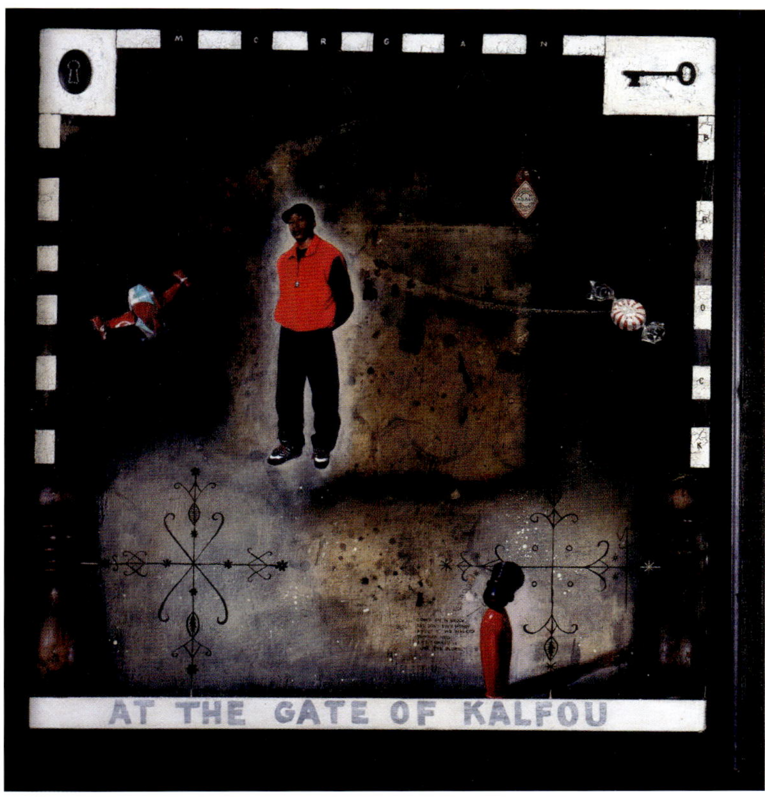

At the Gate of Kalfou 1998

the entrance to the crossroads. The airplane signifies Morgan's journey to the spirit world. During 1998 Stout repeatedly summoned the deity known as Ogún, the Yoruba god of war and iron, who came to the New World with the same name and is honored in the Vodou religion as the father of modern society. Ogún symbolizes progress associated with modern machinery and weapons forged from metal. Stout's father and other members of her family were ironworkers. In *Ogún's Bed*, a life-size construction fabricated from found metal objects, Stout pays homage to her father. The piece incorporates wire, tools, old radiator grates, horseshoes, and chain. According to Robert Farris Thompson, the chain symbolizes Ogún's uniting force.[13] Also completed in 1998 were *Mantle in the House of Ogún* and *Oath to Ogún*. The first is an altarpiece showing reverence to Ogún and asking for his protection. The clock represents the watchful eye of ancestor spirits and the gun symbolizes Ogún's protective power. *Oath to Ogún* combines imagery of the crossroads with the lock and key, the old door handle, the faint shadow of a cross, bright red crosses, and a wheel. The delicate, stuffed cloth hand covered in sawdust denotes the spirit of an ancestor. The portrait of an African-American man sitting in a chair holding a red rose and rosary[14] implies this piece was created as a memorial.

---

[13]Robert Farris Thompson, *Flash of the Spirit* (New York, Random House, 1983) p. 54.

[14]Used in Vodou, believed to ward evil spirits from the remains of a deceased believer. The beads are placed in the deceased person's hands.

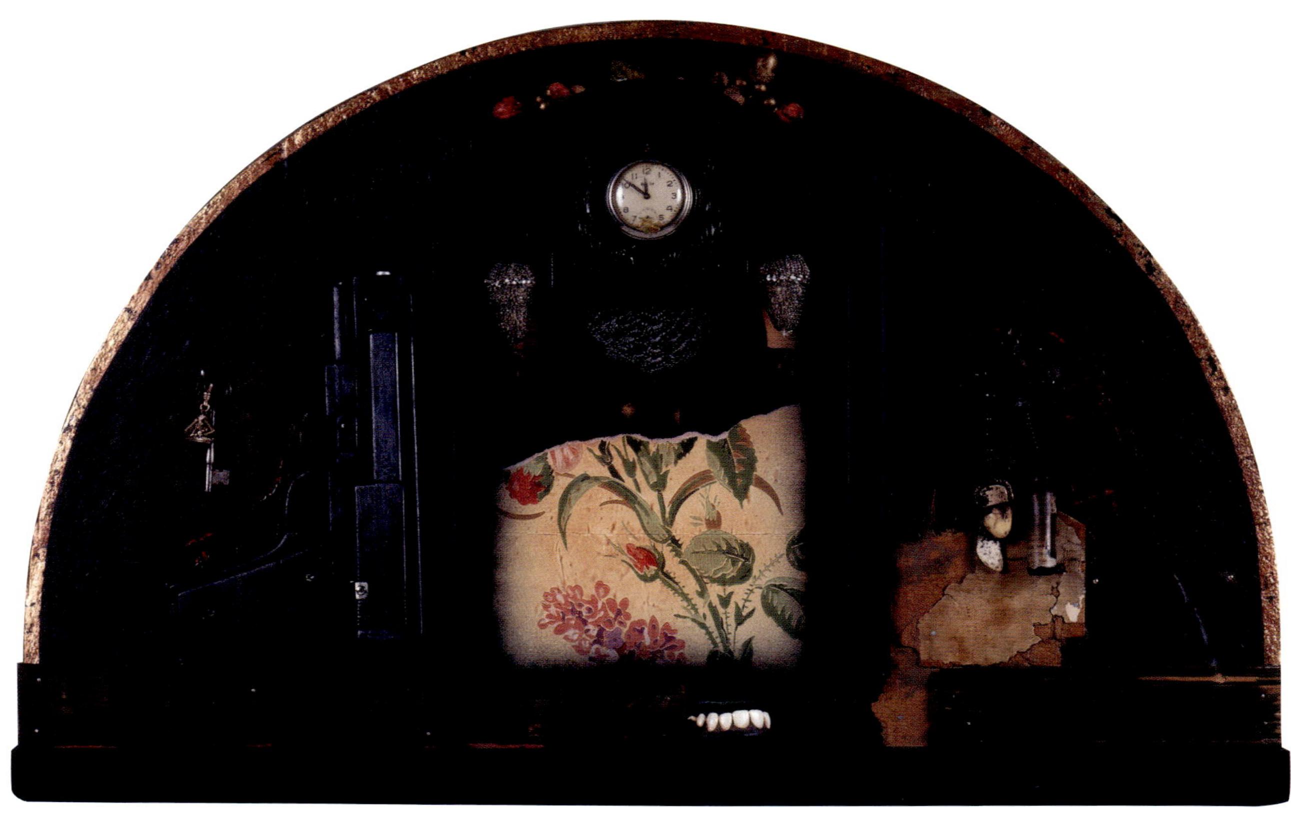

Mantle in the House of Ogún 1998

It is impossible to discuss Stout's work without reference to the American version of Vodou that came from Haiti to New Orleans. Stout visits New Orleans frequently and absorbs its iconoclastic cultural heritage. Louisiana has stronger ties to Haiti than any other state. For many years there was movement of slave owners and slaves between Haiti and New Orleans. In 1804 many free Haitians came to New Orleans after they won independence from France. In 1809 a large number of Haitian planters, who had been refugees in Cuba during the Haitian revolution, were expelled from Cuba and made their way to New Orleans. The influence of Haiti's religious belief system is evident in the strong presence of Vodou rituals in Louisiana. Although Louisiana Vodou is less organized than its Haitian model, it is just as powerful. Both forms of Vodou are influenced by the mysteries of Catholicism, European traditions, and African religious practices. Louisiana Vodou flourished because Africans had some opportunity to practice and keep alive their traditional religious rituals. Some slave owners either did not care about the slave's so-called "savage" private practices or tolerated them when they did not interfere with the work schedule. In 1817 the New Orleans City Council set aside a place for slaves to openly congregate. The area located across from Rampart Street was known as Congo Square.[15] During this time, a native of Haiti, John Montenet,

[15]Known today as Louis Armstrong Park in New Orleans–originally a tract of land set aside for slaves and other blacks to congregate under the watchful eye of city authorities.

became the father of Louisiana Vodou. It is claimed he combined Haitian Vodou, Catholicism, snake worship, and European ideas into the Louisiana blend of Vodou. His reach extended beyond the black community, enticing white women to his "advice parlor" with his listening skills, sure demeanor, and magical potions.

Louisiana Vodou rituals were a flamboyant affair. Members of the cult changed clothes prior to the ceremonies, putting on sandals and tying deep-red handkerchiefs around their waists. The queen wore a red outfit with a red sash, while the splendidly dressed king wore a number of colorful handkerchiefs, a blue waist cord, and "red stuff" on his head. The king served the queen, the dominant figure in the ceremony, making sure it ran smoothly. Elected to her position for life, the queen often was the king's actual wife. Meetings started with the adoration of a snake in a barred cage or on an altar in front of the royal pair. Next was the renewal of the society's oath of secrecy. At some point, the queen-the only person who could be possessed by a spirit-would convulse and talk through "spirit lips"[16] in an unknown tongue while an offering was taken up. Throughout the ritual, celebrants consumed tafia,[17] an intoxicating mixture akin to rum.

[16]Possession in Louisiana Vodou.

[17]Rum and molasses beverage used in Vodou ritual.

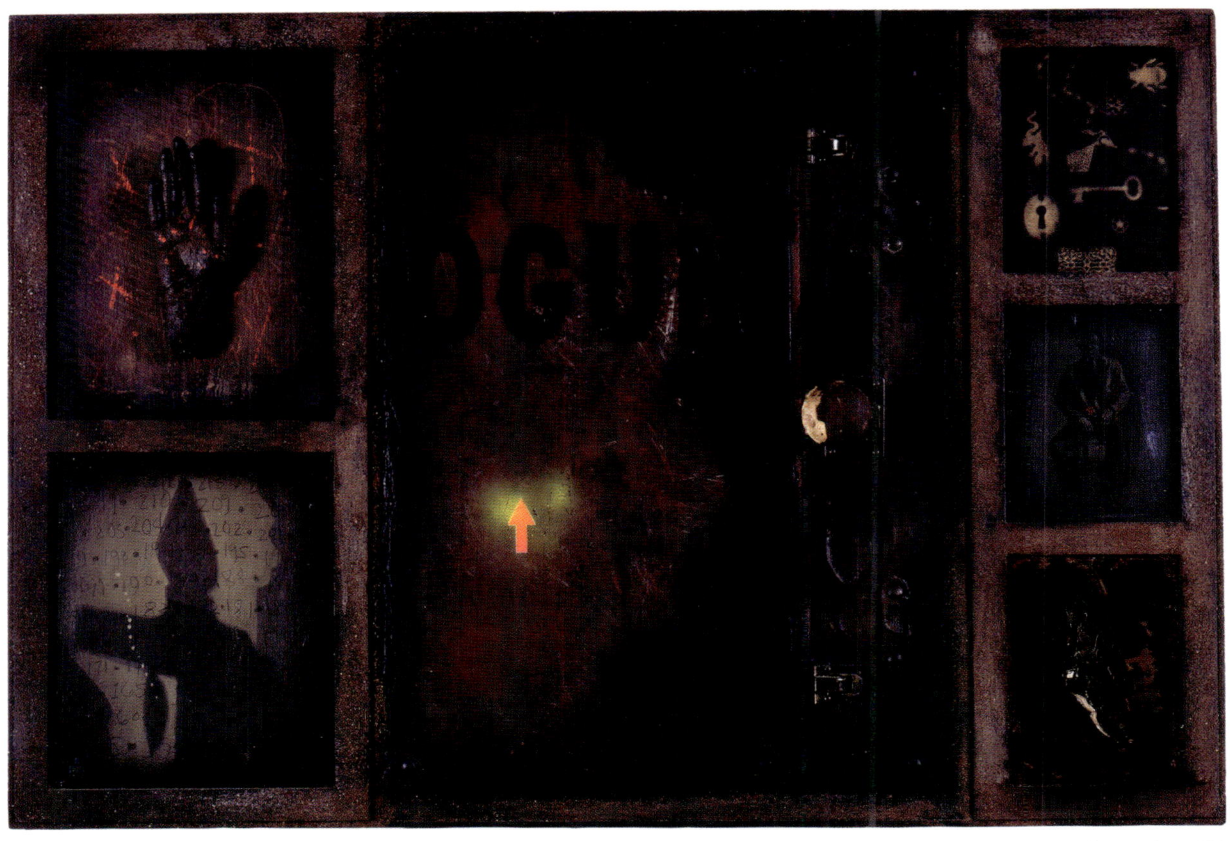

Oath to Ogún 1998

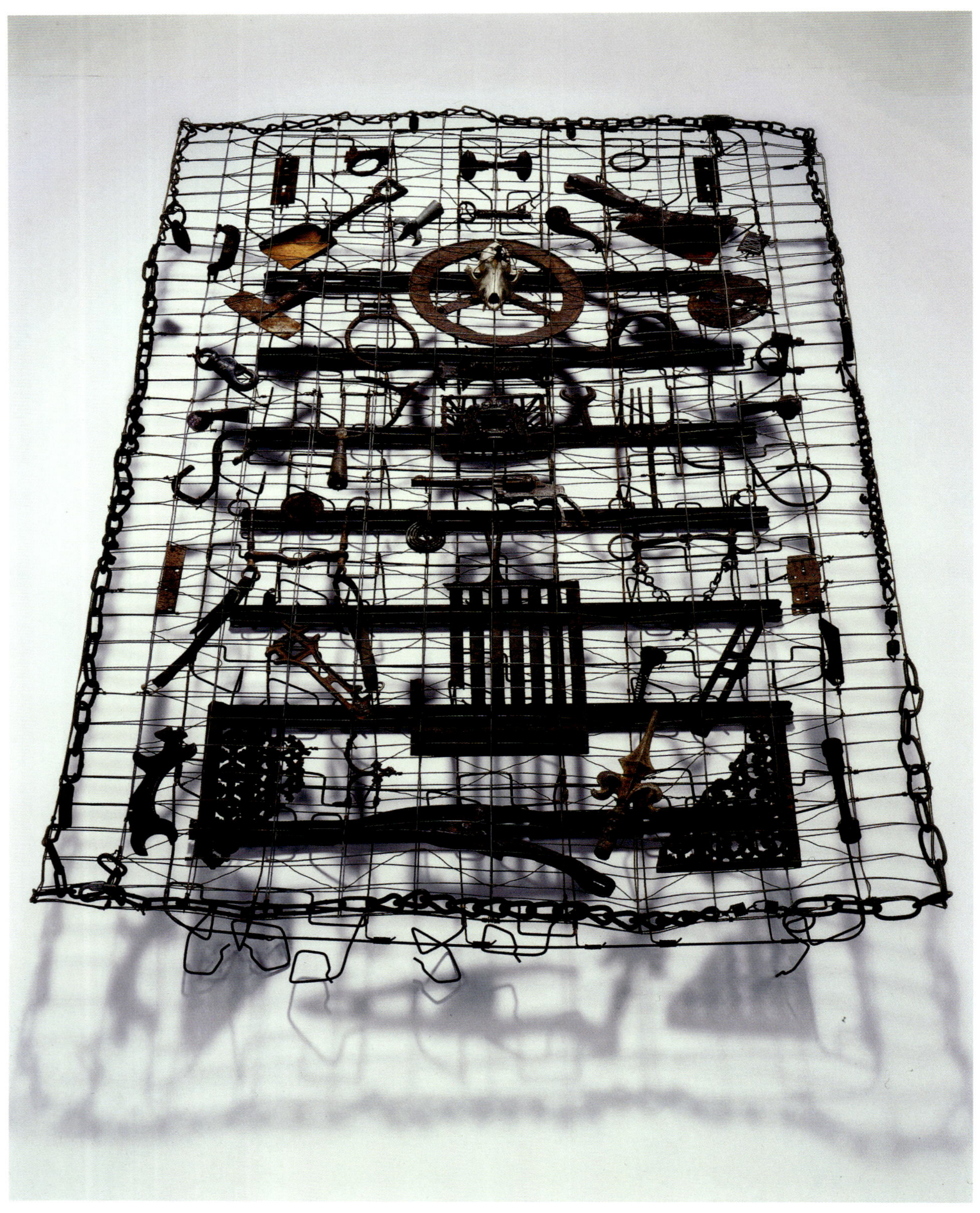

Ogún's Bed 1998

The king traced a large circle in the center of the room with a piece of charcoal and placed offerings to the spirits in the middle. The circle echoes Haitian rituals and served to call the proper spirits to the ceremony.[18]

The best known Louisiana Vodou queen, Marie Laveau, emerged as a priestess in the 1820s. In time she became New Orleans's most powerful Vodou figure and, in the process, put her unique stamp on the religion. Claiming that her followers were Christian, Laveau added statues of saints, prayers, incense, and holy water to the traditional Vodou rites, which had for some time incorporated snakes, a black cat, and roosters. Vodou became increasingly popular during Laveau's reign. After her death, a less open Vodou organization emerged. By the 1920s it was difficult to find any public trace of the once thriving and tightly organized Vodou society. The old ways of practicing Vodou were either no longer needed or no longer acceptable to those wishing to be assimilated into the mainstream of American society. Louisiana Vodou, as practiced in the nineteenth century, went underground to be replaced in the public consciousness by a new, milder, and more commercialized version characterized by the use of spells, tricks, conjurations, witchcraft, and potions. This is the Vodou prevalent in New Orleans today. Only loosely connected to the original practice, it is designed to get favors from the saints or spirits. By the 1940s a number of storefront operations and self-proclaimed healers appeared in the French Quarter of New Orleans. Their boutiques sold potions, charms, and gris-gris,[19] but did not openly practice Vodou rituals.

Stout has incorporated advertisements for Vodou paraphernalia into her art. *Come See Me* offers spiritual supplies and palm readings for a nominal fee. The sign suggests through the image of the key that the store has the power to unlock the door to the crossroads. *Kinley's Drug Store* advertises oils and roots that cure ailments, offering an alternative to modern medicine. "We've got everything you need, if you don't have Medicare, Medicade [sic], or insurance." The Kongo nkisi figure on the left holds herbal remedies in his belly with the sign of the crossroads overhead.

We Do Tattoos (cover) is the ultimate advertisement for the Vodou version of one-stop shopping. The colorful, eye-catching design alerts the customer to the many services available inside the shop. Patrons can cure their ills and ensure love, success, and happiness through an array of powders, oil, and incense. Individual mojos, or charms, can be assembled to any specification and the future can be told through card readings. Spiritual tattoos appear to be an added service, continuing the age-old tradition of body art. In West Africa, scarification is performed for several purposes. Markings may have protective, as

---

[18]Maya Deren, *Divine Horsemen.*

[19]A potion, or charm, used to ward off bad luck. It is often a bag containing herbs, hair, and nail clippings.

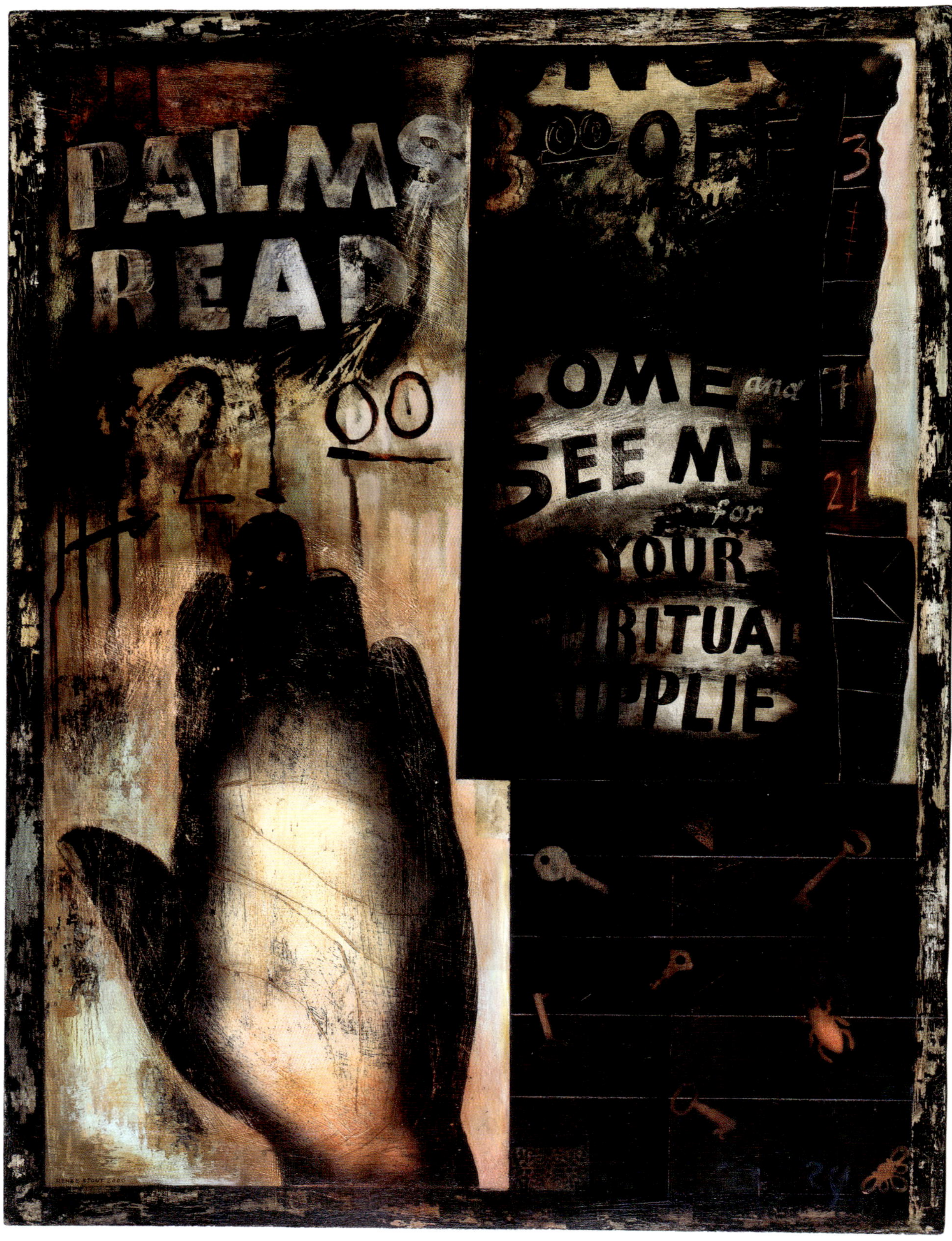

Come See Me 2000

well as aesthetic and identifying qualities. Culturally, the practice dates back thousands of years, and has been used to identify tribes or groups and individual family clusters. Scars also served as beauty marks. In pre-Columbian America, tattoos were used for similar purposes as African scarification. According to Stout, her grandfather's two sisters had Indian heads tattooed on their backs. A New Orlean's artist Stout knows said the Indian heads could denote healers.

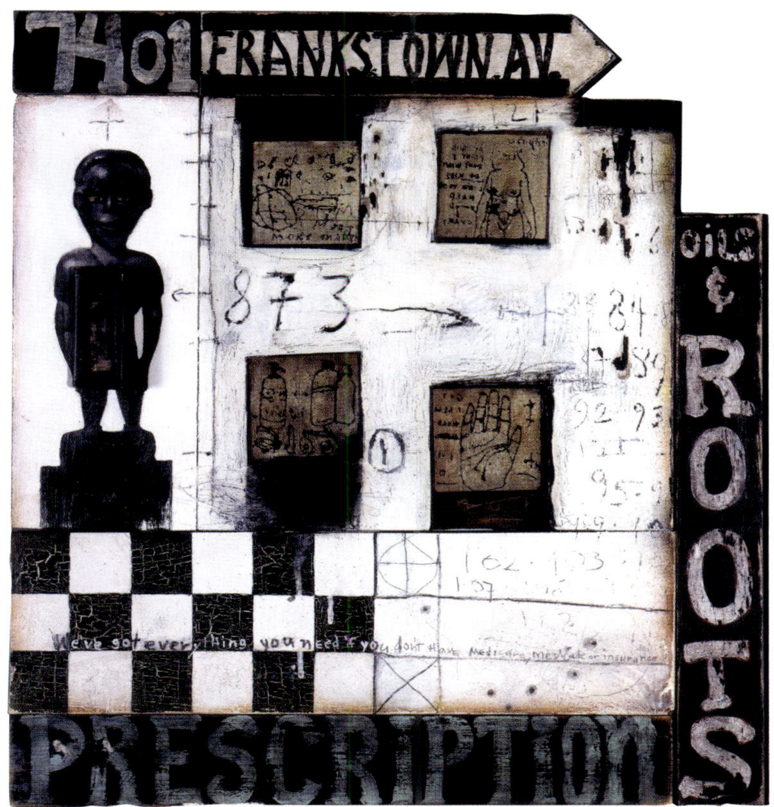

Kinley's Drug Store 1999

Stout combines all of Vodou's spiritual elements in her work, bringing to life the rituals and the process of self-healing by creating imaginary characters and scenarios. These fictional characters accompany the artist, appearing in different works to produce vivid narratives that capture the viewer's imagination. According to Stout, these characters are the vehicles through which she works out conflicting aspects of her own personality. Madam Ching is one such character who reappears and aids the artist in her quest for love and happiness. The inspiration for this character comes from an old conjure-woman who lived in Pittsburgh. Her window had a painted sign that read simply, "Madam Ching." Stout never knew Madam Ching but the atmosphere of secrecy and eccentricity around her was so intriguing it stimulated the artist's imagination. Over a six year period, Stout created numerous works that centered on Madam Ching.

Stout's Madam Ching is loosely based on the Haitian Loa, Erzulie, the goddess of love and lust. The Yoruba refer to her as Oshun and in the New World she became Erzulie. She personifies gentle affection, devotion, and friendship, as well as desire, raw sensuality, and an insatiable sexual appetite. She is the earth mother and, as stated earlier, strongly identified with the Virgin Mary, whose symbol is a heart. Erzulie has a taste for the exquisite and surrounds herself with expensive perfumes, delicate lace, and fresh flowers. Her colors are blue, red, and gold. The color gold equals "essence, refinement of the light;" gold from the earth is like light from the sun.[20] Stout used Erzulie's attributes and in

[20]Alvia Wardlaw, Robert V. Rozelle, and Maureen A, McKenna, eds., *Black Art/Ancestral Legacy: The African Impulse in African-American Art* (Dallas, Dallas Museum of Art, 1989) p. 109.

nearly all the pieces associated with Madam Ching. She appeared in Stout's art at a time when the artist was discovering herself and dealing with relationship issues in her personal life. Stout's Madam Ching is a root-worker whose specialty is love. The artist recreates items from her store to give the viewer insights into the life of a healer. It is as if the viewer has secretly entered the store in Madam Ching's absence. The owner's physical identity will forever be a mystery; but bits of paper detailing the ingredients for Vodou potions and various herbs and oils scattered around the store reveal the healer's methods and materials.

Traveling Root Store exhibits just a few of Madam Ching's various ingredients. Hanging from a coat rack is the healer's exquisitely sewn *Conjuring Vest*. It is made with a rich velvet embellished with hundreds of sequins and beads. Mirrors that offer Ching protection line the front closure, while individual charms conceal protective writing and cover the vest's surface. Mysterious appliquéd symbols also adorn the vest, whose design recalls West African charm vests. There, priests would add charms to their vests over the course of a lifetime. Considered sacred, these garments were often buried with their owner. It is easy to imagine Madam Ching dressed in her conjuring vest working diligently at her desk, preparing various

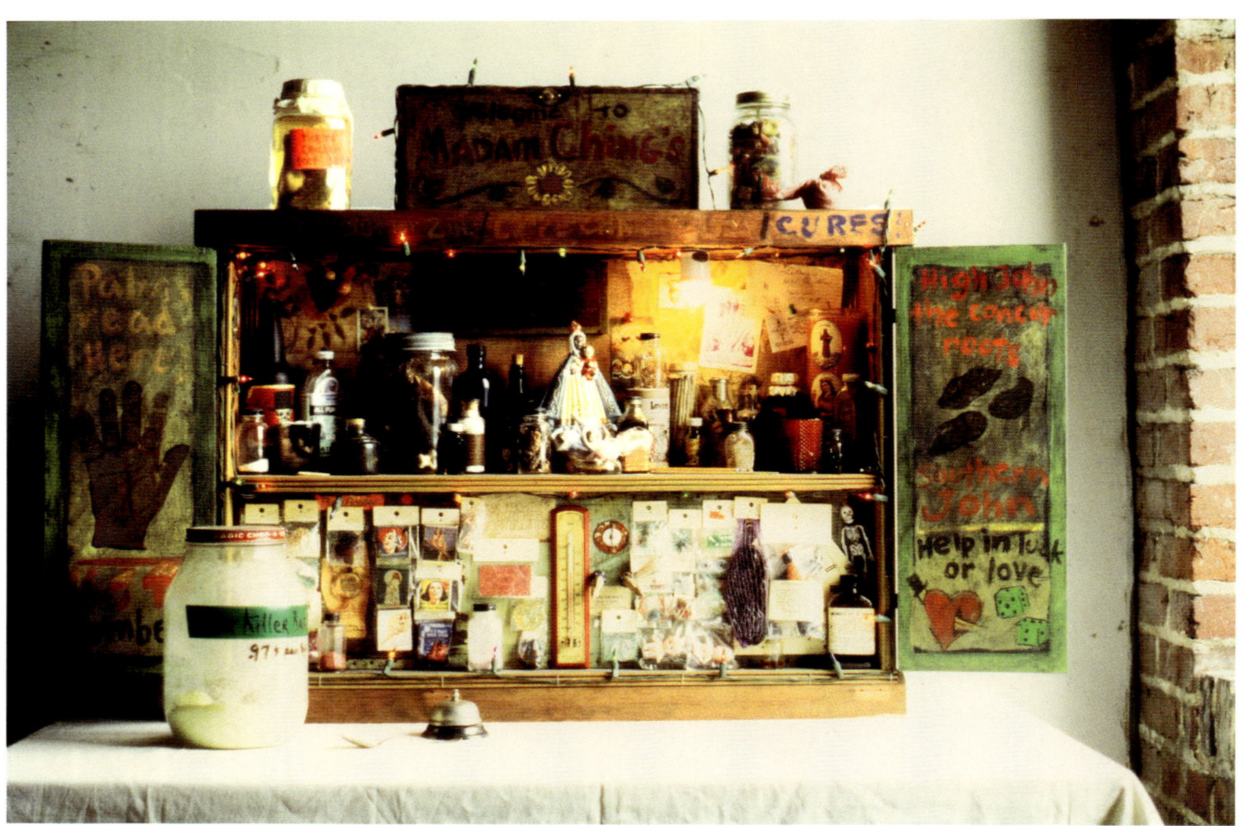

Traveling Root Store 1995

potions and charms for her devoted patrons. A *trompe l'oeil* hand suggests she also reads palms and two playing cards imply her skill as a card reader, as well. Her special love potion, "Sensitivity Potion," is prominently displayed in a large glass bottle with a beaded lid. It instructs users to just follow the directions on the bottle: "Ladies, sprinkle 5 drops into any light colored food . . . within 5 days your man will show an increased sensitivity to your needs and desires." To honor Erzulie, an antique beveled-glass frame showcases her veve symbol, encrusted with glitter, sequins, and beads. Two cosmograms, or crosses, flank either side summoning Erzulie's spirit. The birth date 1916 pays homage to Stout's grandmother.

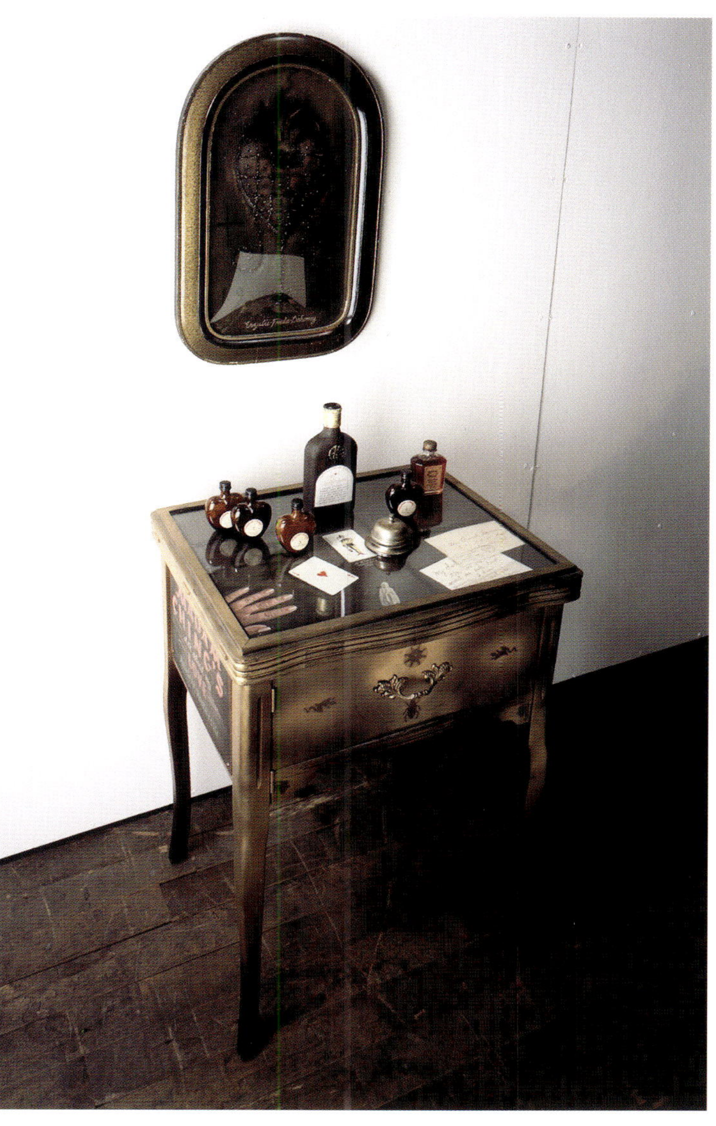

Madam Ching's Love Products 1995

Love Charm #2 casts a spell designed to capture another's heart and body. A pink powder representing love is sprinkled over a frog's leg bones, symbolizing Stout's male love interest. The bottle is locked within a wooden box decorated with the Haitian veve for Erzulie. String binds the hinges and a tied root is chained to the box. Inscribed crosses appear on all sides of the box summoning the Loa. This charm's physical construction implies that Stout would like to ensure that her love interest stays true to her at all costs. In both African and New World traditions the action of tying a charm binds the owner of the charm to the intended. The root, incorporating many levels of symbolic meaning, can be construed to represent life, love, or a phallus. Maybe Madam Ching has devised a charm to control all three.

When not at her root store, Madam Ching can create charms and potions on location with *Traveling Root Store #2*, a portable conjuring bag. The case is a vintage suitcase found in a local furniture store. Although most of the contents are traditional ingredients, the computer establishes Madam Ching as a twentieth-century healer. Stout filled the case with every imaginable charm, root, herb, and potion. It also contains a bottle of jinx remover, attraction bath, protective doll charm, snakeskin, and a horn charm, all ingredients required by a conjurer-woman on the go. The computer

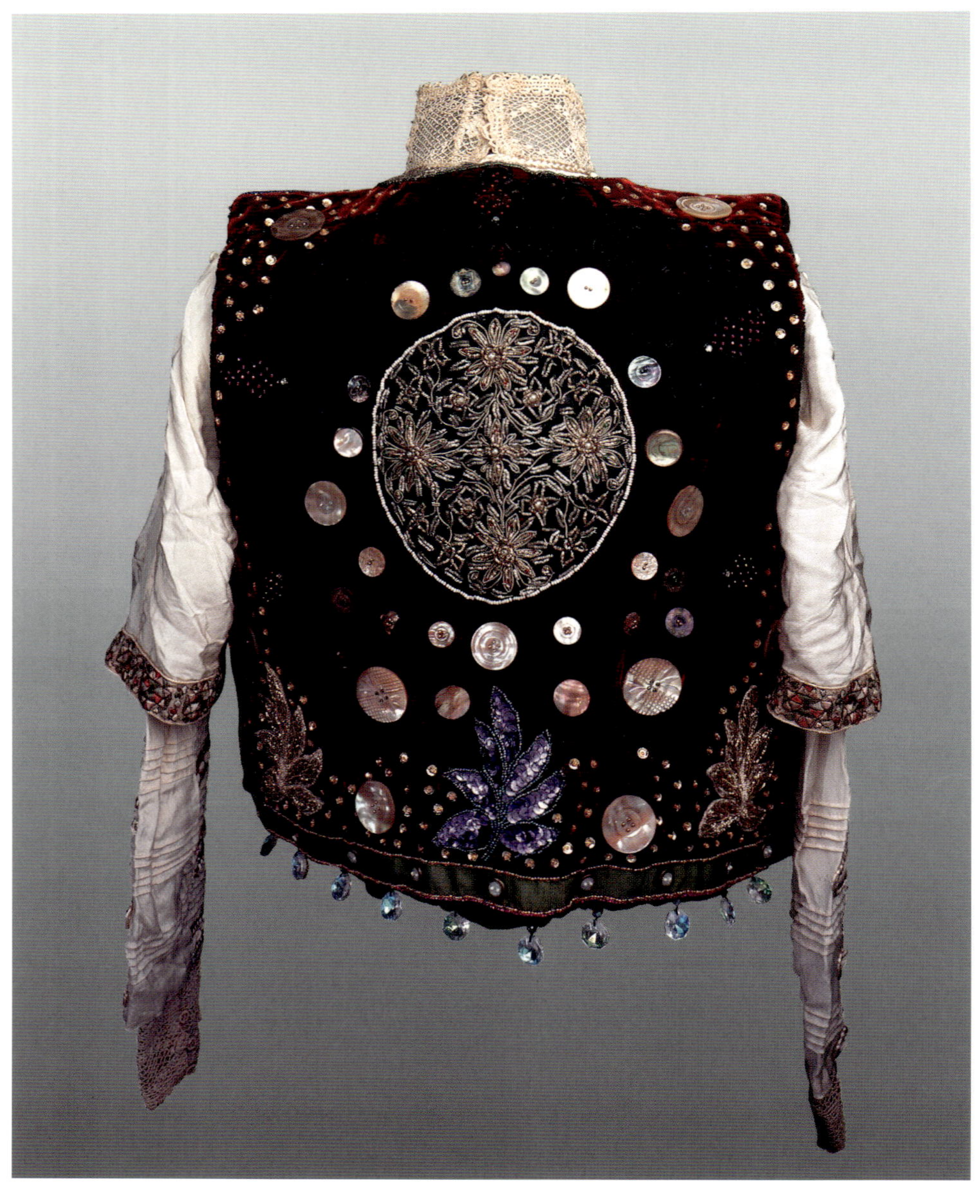

Conjuring Vest 1996

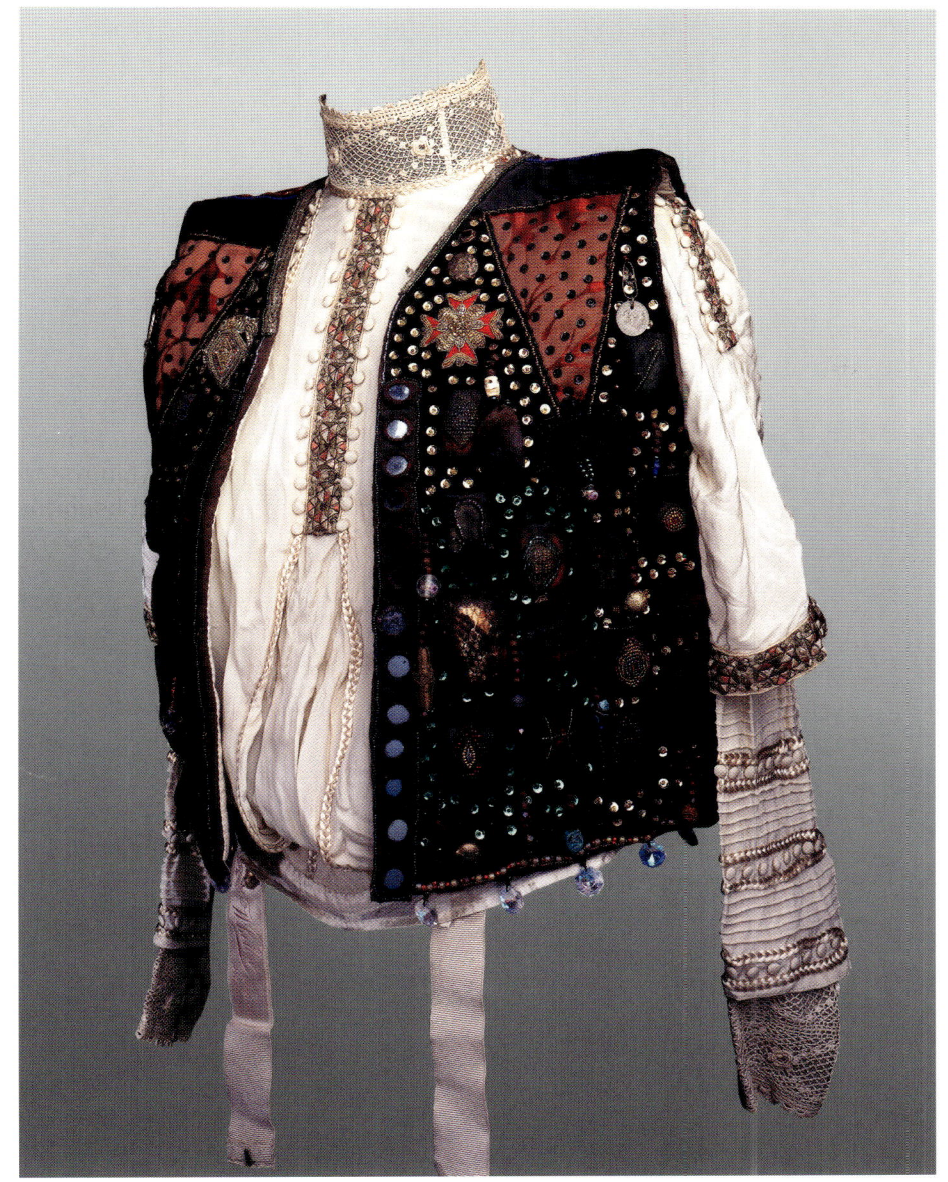

Conjuring Vest 1996

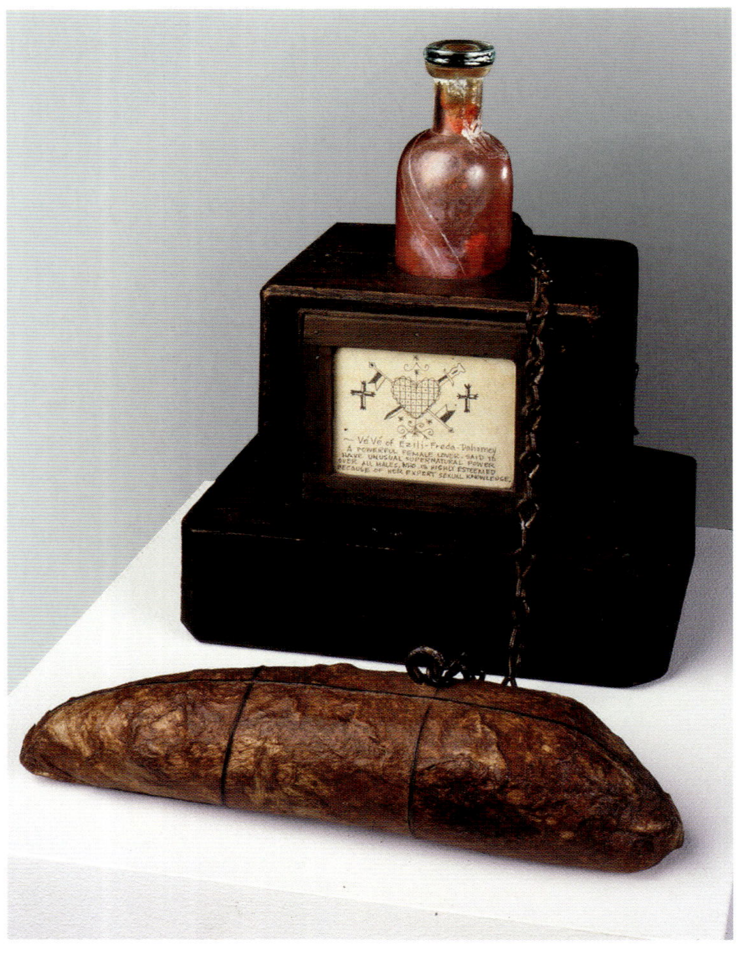

Love Charm #2 1994

placed in the middle has been altered to meet Madam Ching's conjuring needs. For example, Ching can transcend the past, present, and future at the touch of a button. On the screen is a spell that has been e-mailed by Erzulie. It includes four pink candles, one yellow candle, and aphrodisia incense. It appears that the goddess of love has just given Madam Ching a powerful attraction potion. When the viewer encounters the suitcase, the screen has been left on, but Madam Ching is nowhere to be found. Has she transcended into the past or crossed over into the future? Neither Stout nor Madam Ching's clients will ever know the answer.

Bibliography

Berns, Marla C., ***Dear Robert, See You at the Crossroads***, Santa Barbara, The Regents of the University of California University Art Museum, 1995.

Deren, Maya. ***Divine Horsemen, The Living Gods of Haiti,*** New York, McPherson & Company, 1953.

Gleason, Judith. ***Oya, In Praise of the Goddess.*** Boston, Shambhala Publications, Inc., 1987.

Harris, Michael D. ***Astonishment and Power, Resonance, Transformation, and Rhyme,*** Washington D.C., Smithsonian Institution, 1993.

Haskins, Jim. ***VooDoo and HooDoo,*** Scarborough House, 1990.

Thompson, Robert Farris. ***Flash of the Spirit,*** New York, Random House, 1983.

Thompson, Robert Farris and Joseph Cornet. ***Four Moments of the Sun: Kongo Art in Two Worlds,*** Washington D.C., National Gallery of Art, 1981.

Wardlaw, Alvia, Robert V. Rozelle, and Maureen A. McKenna, eds., ***Black Art/Ancestral Legacy: The African Impulse in African-American Art,*** (Dallas, Dallas Museum of Art, 1989).

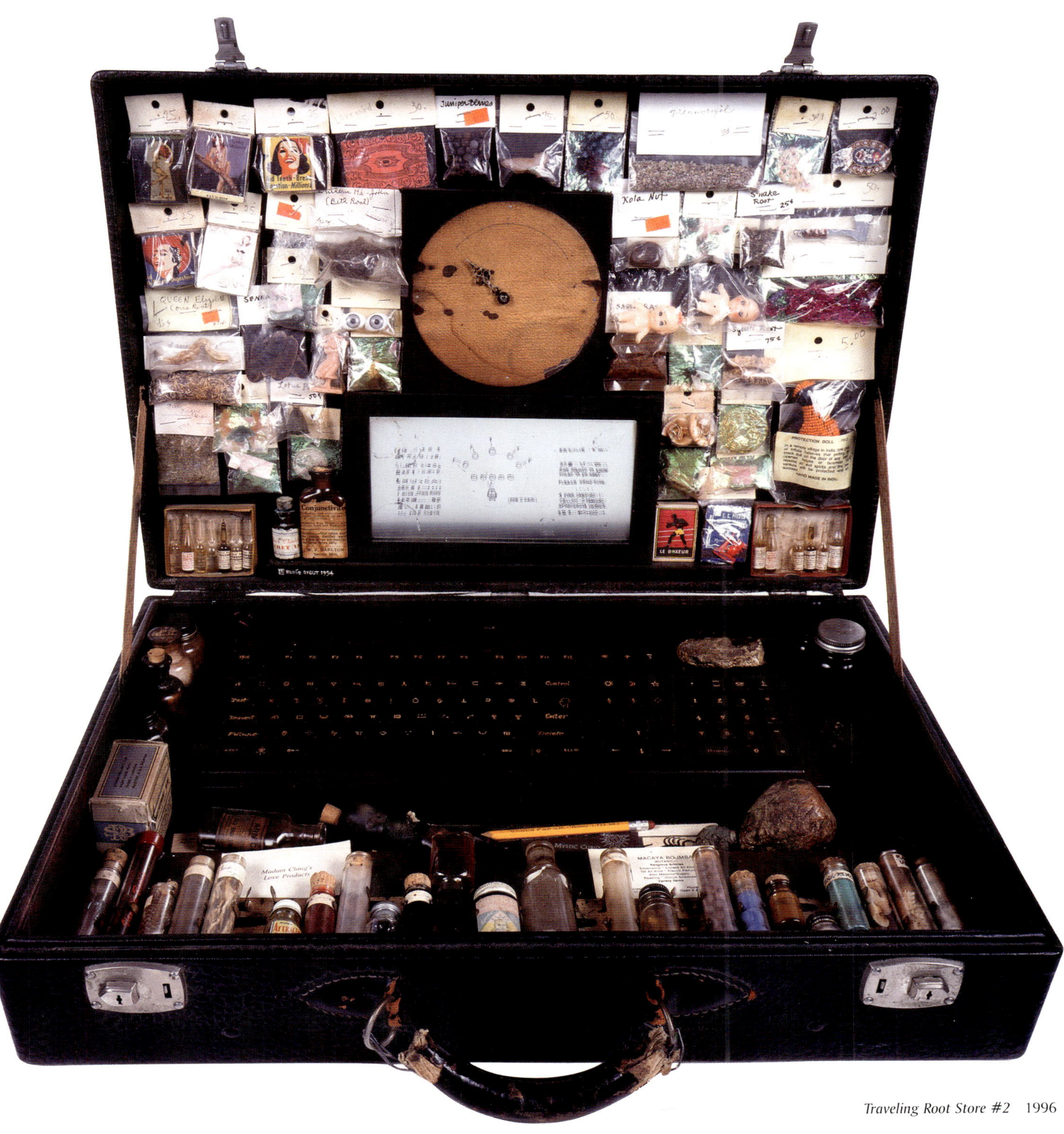

Traveling Root Store #2 1996

List of Terms

Yoruba - Black Africa's largest population whose territory encompasses Western Nigeria and eastern Republic of Benin. Their extensive spiritual pantheon contains thousands of deities. Yoruba religious beliefs strongly influenced Haitian Vodou with many of the spirits' individual characteristics remaining the same.

Divination - Ceremonial ritual designed to communicate with the spirit world through inanimate objects. The Yoruba throw kola nuts and cast cowrie shells. The placement of the objects once they land is interpreted by a priest and considered the will of the spirits. All problems are solved through some form of divination.

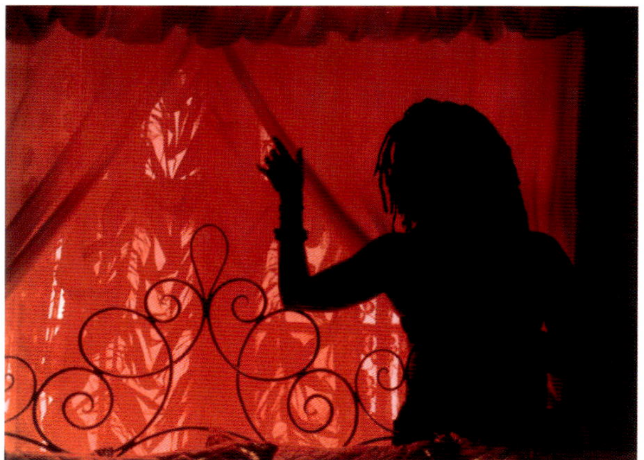

Kongo - Peoples from West Africa who greatly influenced black religions because of their numerous population in the New World. Their central belief system is based on the cosmogram.

Cosmogram - A Kongo cross symbolizing the cycle of life, which they believe never ends and represents the recycling of the soul. The horizontal line divides the land of the living from the land of the dead.

Crossroads - A central Vodou image derived from the cosmogram. It is the place where the worlds of earth and spirit meet. Virtually all Vodou acts, even healing, begin with the acknowledgment of the crossroads.

Possession - Loa often attend a Vodou ceremony or ritual and take possession of the priest or priestess, departing its human host after possession. Individuals do not remember what happened during possession.

Veve - ceremonial drawings done on the ground in flour or cornmeal symbolically depicting the various Loa before a ceremony.

Loa - Spirits in the Haitian Vodou pantheon. Each serves various functions in the universe. (Example: Loa of agriculture, Loa of death). Loa can also be the spirits of dead family members.

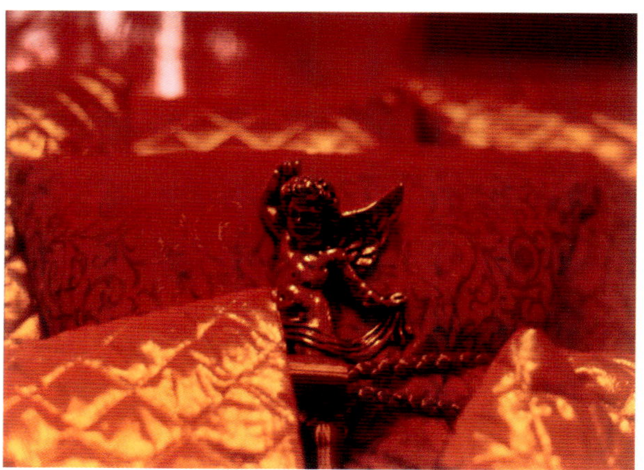

Houngan - A male Vodou priest. Only a houngan can summon a Loa, and therefore they are the only people capable of influencing life and the future.

Papa Ghede/Baron Samedi - Loa of death and resurrection and protector of children. His symbol is a cross placed over the tomb.

Elegba/Legba - Loa who is the guardian of the crossroads, as well as the messenger between mortals and the spirit world.

Ogún - Loa of war and iron giving followers strength through prophecy and aiding in political strife.

Damballah - Loa who is the master of all waters, whose symbol is the snake.

Erzulie - Loa of love and lust represented by a heart and identified with the Virgin Mary.

John Montenet - Haitian-born New Orleans Vodou practitioner believed to have first integrated traditional Vodou ways with elements of Catholicism and the snake oracle.

High John the Conqueror root - A root sold in local pharmacies and used in Vodou rites to obtain the assistance of High John, protector of blacks.

Gris-gris - A potion, or charm, used to ward off bad luck. It is often a bag containing herbs, hair, and nail clippings.

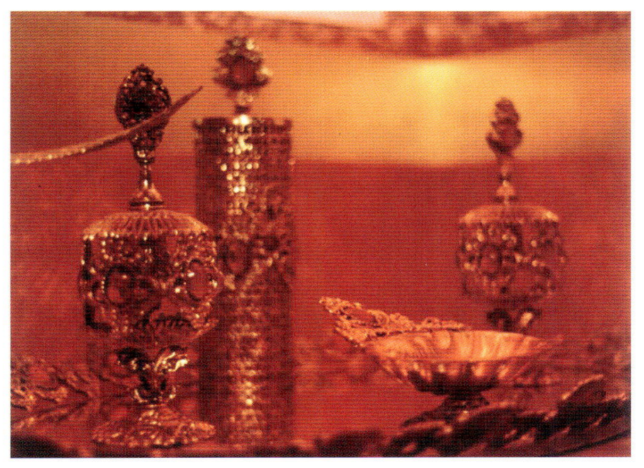

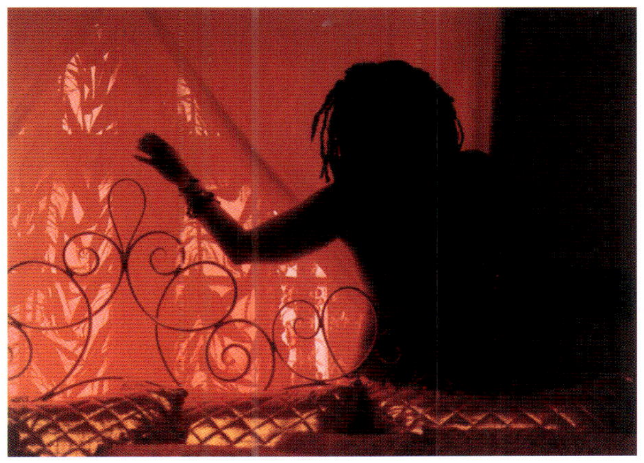

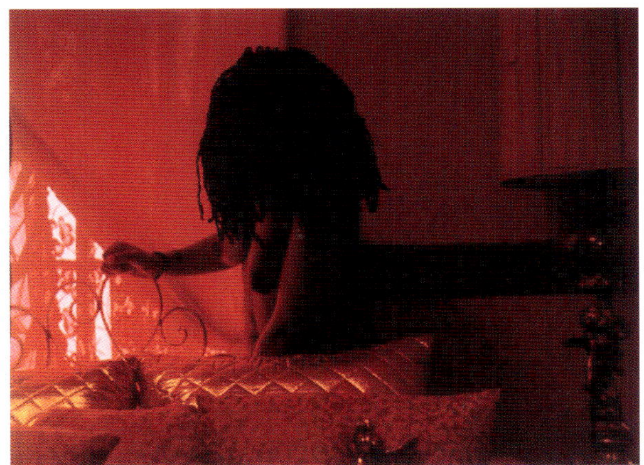

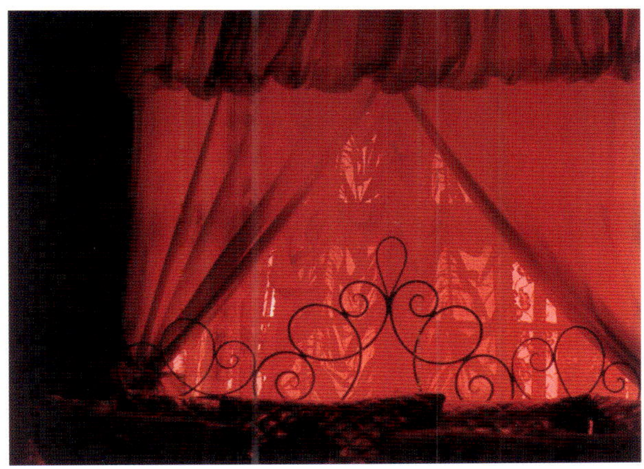

The Red Room 1997

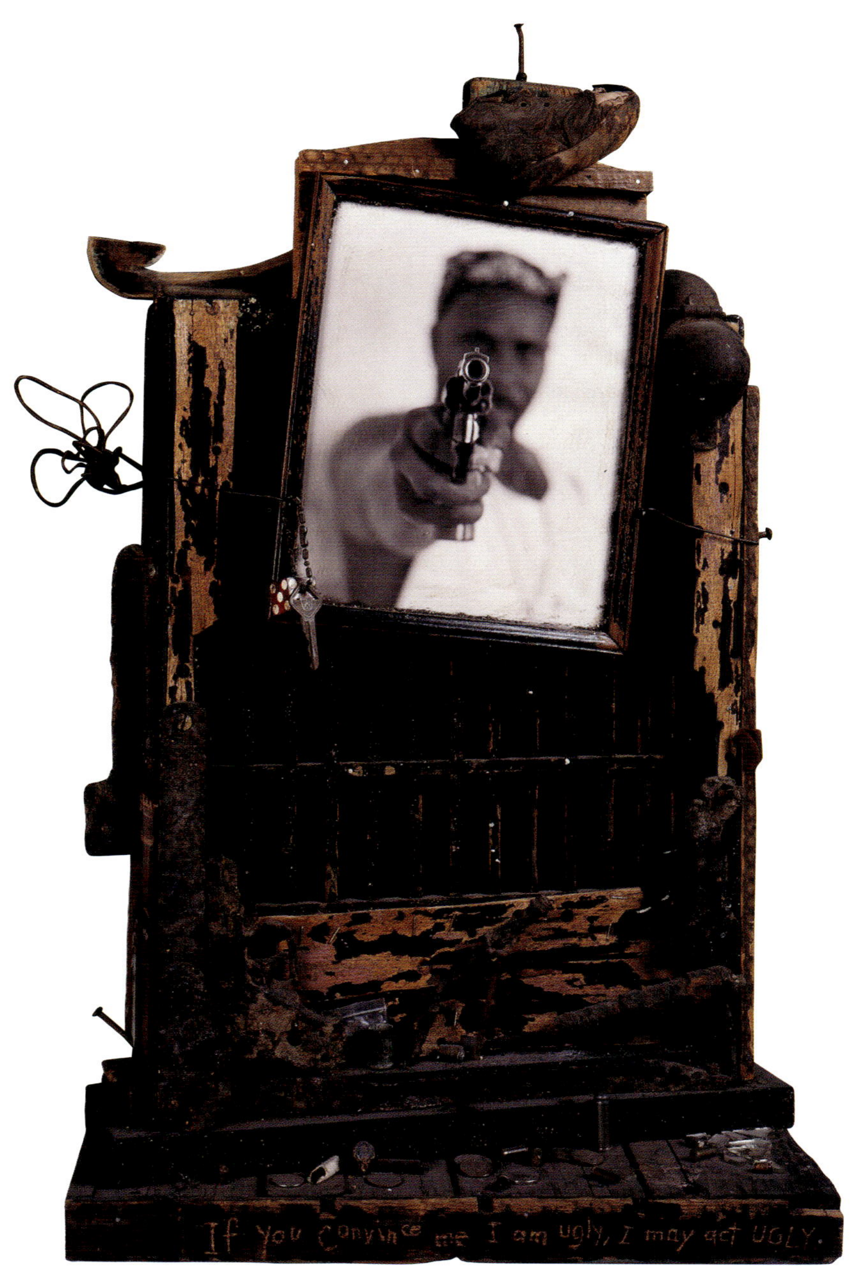
If you Convince me I am ugly, I may act UGLY.

Awakening

Stephen Bennett Phillips

Growing up in Pittsburgh, Renée Stout was more interested in art than current events. During the 1960s, Pittsburgh was not segregated, so she could go anywhere. Her family lived in a racially mixed neighborhood and she attended an integrated grade school. Born in 1958, Stout was too young to have more than vague recollections of the civil rights movement and only a few memories of the Vietnam War protests. Her first memory of a political event dates to 1963 when her father explained President Kennedy's assassination. Two years later, she heard about urban riots, looting, and burning. She also remembers driving with her family one day, when her mother pointed out a group of Black Panthers wearing black leather. She learned of Dr. Martin Luther King's murder in 1968 from watching the news. Stout remembers that by the end of the decade, she thought that strange things were going on but she didn't know why.

The significance of Stout's Pittsburgh upbringing can be seen in her belief that class, not race, is the main social issue. In fact, Pittsburgh's major political battles were fought around labor issues, including the efforts in 1969 to desegregate the trades unions, leading to boycotts. Stout believes that if working people of all ethnic groups realized how much they have in common, the issue of race would disappear. In 1972 Stout took up her first political cause: the fourteen-year-old wore a large "Free Angela Davis" button for several months until the black activist, wrongly accused of murder, was acquitted. At the time, Stout did not consider herself a political activist but, like most teenagers, she had a deep desire for justice. This would show up later in her ideas and artwork.

When Stout moved to Washington in August 1985, with President Ronald Reagan in his second term, she became aware of how the political system works. Being "smack in the middle of the most political city in the world," she began to "connect the dots," as she said, and came to realize how politics and policies affect different communities in dissimilar ways. She found it hard to see the much-vaunted benefits of the current economic "trickle down" theory on the streets. Instead, Stout saw the rich getting richer, while everyone else struggled. For the first time, she realized that politics was more marketing than action. Moral contradictions became obvious to Stout: failure of a supposedly Christian country to follow Christian ethics and charity; failure to help the less fortunate; and triumphant self-interest. Stout ceased believing the rhetoric about the United States being a great country, because the people who most needed help were those least likely to get it.

In 1994 Stout gained first-hand experience of the plight of the downtrodden when she moved into the first of four spaces on O Street in Northwest D.C. The O Street Studios were located in a depressed neighborhood and had many artists as residents. The neighborhood also attracted a colorful mix of transients including

Opposite page:
Point of View 1994
(front view)

homeless people, drug dealers, and prostitutes. An organization called SOME (So Others Might Eat) was located just across the street. Stout found the sight of hungry men and women lining up to eat each day, early in the morning, very powerful. The neighborhood was also an open-air drug market selling heroin in the 1980s and crack by the time Stout moved in. She saw firsthand how drugs were devastating the community, both by watching people on the street always looking for a fix and by seeing friends going through rehab. Coming and going to and from her studio, Stout began to recognize the people who hung out on her block and soon became cordial with several of them. She saw that they were people whose needs were not being considered by the politicians. Through the early and mid-1990s, Stout's political ideas came into focus and she became more of an activist. She marched for woman's rights, abortion rights, and gay rights and continued to pay close attention to current events. As she absorbed information, Stout made sure to think between the lines, because she knew the media slant was not always accurate.

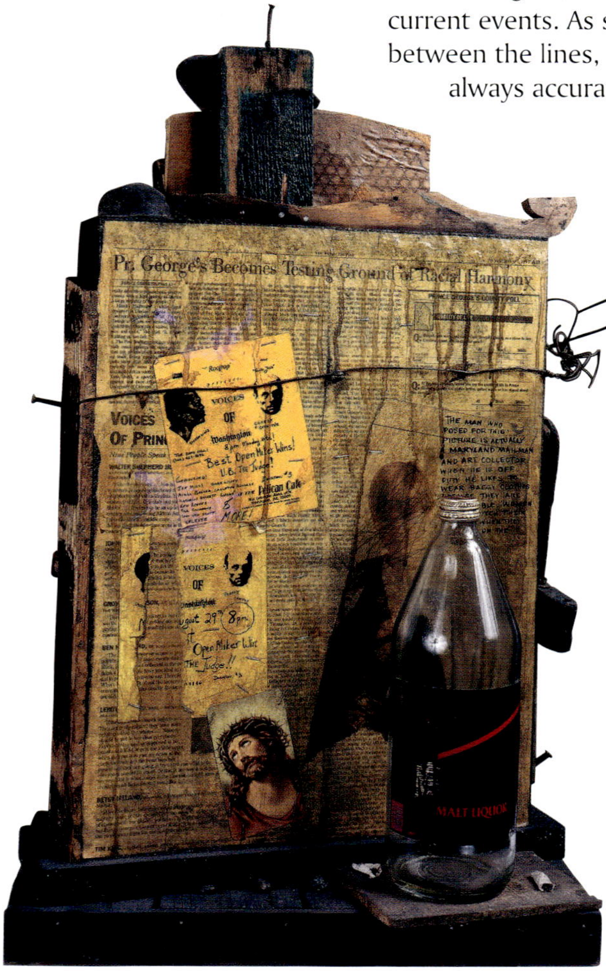

Point of View 1994
(back view)

Point of View, an aggressive and confrontational three-dimensional piece, is the first work in which Stout began to deal with some of her political ideas. The work addresses the fact that the media in general, and especially television, do not present an accurate picture of people, especially African-Americans and other ethnic groups. In the work, the most powerful element—a man holding a gun that follows wherever the viewer turns—is foremost. To create the work, Stout posed a friend holding a gun. She purposefully made the photograph look blurred. Around it she placed rusty and worn-out items. At the top is a baby's shoe that signifies how the streets have worn out children because they have seen everything by the time they become adults. At the bottom of the piece, she alludes to an alley littered with objects such as a rusty old gun, bullet casings, a crack bag, cigarette butts, small change, and shards of mirror glass. At the bottom an inscription reads: "If you convince me that I am ugly, I may act ugly." On the back, Stout placed an empty bottle of malt liquor, because it is primarily marketed to the African-American community with names such as Colt .45 and Magnum .40, also the names of guns, thus promoting violence in the community. The collage, also on the back, includes the story of the man in the photograph: "The man who posed for this picture is actually a Maryland mailman and art collector. When he is off duty he likes to wear baggy clothes because they are comfortable. Women often clutch their purses when they pass him on the sidewalk." Stout's point is that many young blacks watch the media's portrayal of their race and buy into negative stereotype. In a way, it gives these kids a license to act out, thereby fitting right into the media image of them. In Stout's mind, the media create a self-fulfilling prophecy and are ultimately responsible for many of the problems they report.

From 1997 to 1998, Stout's work focused almost exclusively on her political ideas. This period coincided with the height of Washington's inner-city violence. On O Street, Stout either witnessed or heard about so many people being killed that it was impossible not to feel angry and upset. One day, in her studio, she heard four shots. Jumping up she looked out the window and saw a boy on a bike pulling his hand back and speeding away, leaving another boy in a car slumped over the steering wheel. This was the first time she saw someone killed. She sat down on the floor and cried. Over time she saw how the frequency of these tragedies numbed people in the neighborhood, allowing them to cope with the frequency of the violence. She constantly thought about the problems around her, but she could not always talk about her feelings. Most people did not think about it, she believed, because the carnage was not happening in their backyard. Her feelings found their way into her work.

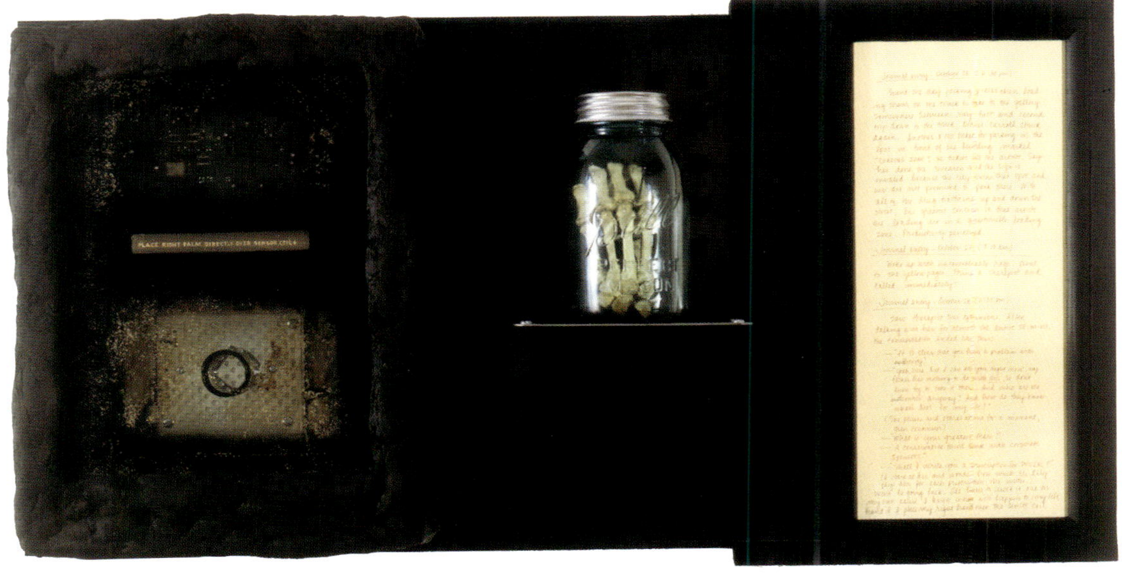

Process of Disassociation 1997

Process of Disassociation deals directly with the way people distance themselves from their emotions when something horrible happens. On July 3, 1997, she heard six loud pops. Since it was the day before the Fourth of July, she first thought it was firecrackers. But down the street a teenage boy whom she had befriended was being killed. What she remembers most about that night was watching his friends express no emotional reaction. Instead, they acted very matter of fact, as though this was life. Stout realized that these kids had gone through a process of disassociation. It hit her that the politicians were not seeing what really happens on the street. They could talk the rhetoric, but they really did not understand what was happening in the urban neighborhoods and why young people were so angry and destructive. She believed these kids were looking for adults to take control of the situation and change it, which was not happening. In response to the absence of adults, kids created their own laws and their own systems to enable them to function within the larger world.

This idea can be seen in *At the Gate of Kalfou*, a work that emerged from the death of another neighborhood friend, Larry Morgan. At the center of the composition is a portrait of the young man. Stout created it by color photocopying a photograph and enhancing it with acrylic paints. Morgan is dressed in a hip-hop outfit in red and black, the colors of Legba–the god of the crossroads who admits mortals to the next plane. The trickster Legba is represented here by the little figure in black and red at the bottom right. Stout positioned toys and candy around Morgan, to show that he is still a young kid, and a bottle of hot sauce for his spicy spirit. He is standing at the gate of Kalfou, another name for the crossroads, here represented by the ornamental iron design in the bottom part of the work. Morgan will put the key at the top right in the keyhole at the top left and open the door to pass through the crossroads from the mortal plane into the spiritual world. After finishing the work, Stout wanted to show Morgan's friends that something constructive could come out of his murder and invited them to look at the painting. Only one accepted the invitation. For Stout, this showed the hardness that had become part of their nature.

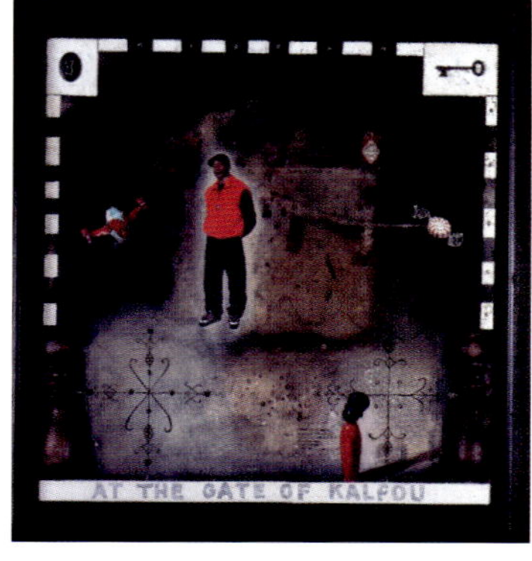

At the Gate of Kalfou 1998

Carpetbagger Politician Goes for a Free Ride on Homeless Woman goes to the root of Stout's attitude about politicians. Inspiration came from the sight of homeless people wandering the streets, pushing shopping carts piled high with their belongings. Stout sees some of these carts as works of art, installation pieces with odd medleys of personal objects tied or stacked up inside. To replicate the visual experience, Stout affixed various objects to the side of her cart: rags, dried oranges, an Nkisi-inspired charm, an image of a black Virgin Mary, locks of hair, and a mannequin's hand. In her effort to hide the interior of the cart, she ripped and knotted her materials, creating an effect of overall patterning. Later, Stout read that knotting is a way to dispel tension.

The idea conveyed by *Carpetbagger Politician Goes for a Free Ride on Homeless Woman* is that politicians are in their own world, talking their rhetoric, but out of touch with everyday reality. To Stout they are basically leeches living off the public instead of contributing by making some real changes. Here, the specific reference is to Lauch Faircloth, a conservative senator then up for re-election. Shown in the center of the cart, the politician has a marzipan pig around his neck and the center seal of a dollar bill stitched to his head. He does no work. Instead, he is wheeled around by the poor. He has two faces, one on the front and one on the back, covered by a stocking mask, indicating that he is really a bandit.

Opposite page:
Carpetbagger Politician Goes for a Free Ride on Homeless Woman 1998

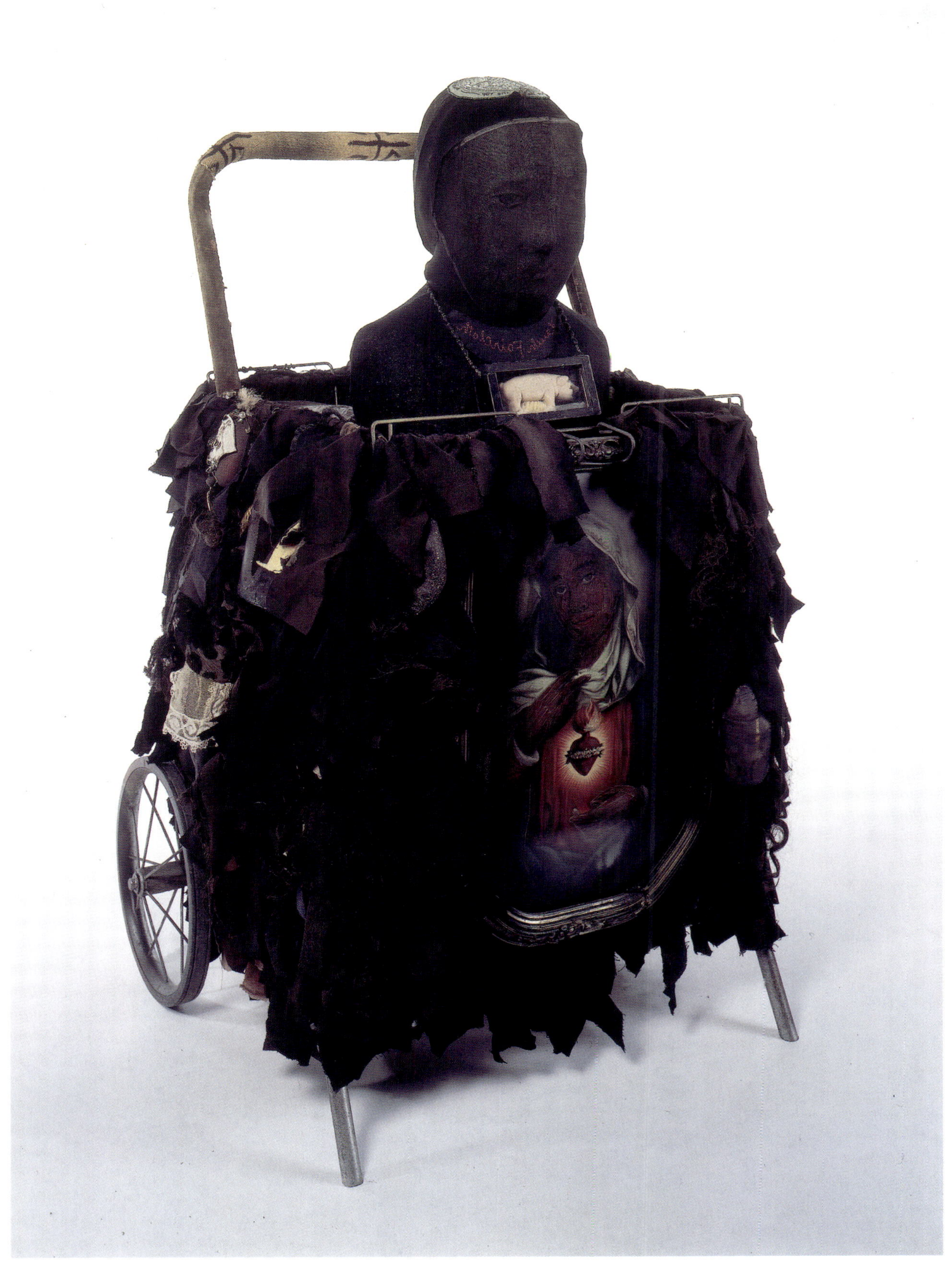

Hoodoo'd to Jesse Helms (p. 55) stems from Stout's distaste for another North Carolina politician. Working on the piece, Stout read a hoodoo poem by a friend, Ernesto Mercer. She felt it matched exactly her ideas about Helms. Mercer, as it turned out, had been thinking about Helms when he wrote the poem and was happy to let her include it in the artwork. Stout found an old mirror and sandpapered some of the silver off and placed the poem in the frame. The piece picks up on some of the images in the poem: "Your teeth are forsaken gravestones . . . your penis is a beheaded rooster that only crows when the sun goes down . . . your heart bristles rusted nails."

Headstone for the Gang of 8 1997

Headstone for the Gang of 8 argues that economic summits organized to set future directions for the entire world include representatives from only a certain group of countries. Originally, the group was made up of the United States, England, Germany, Italy, France, Canada, and Japan. Russia was recently added but is only invited if it remains on good terms with the others, which is why the "8" is crossed out and replaced with a "7." Stout thinks these economic summits openly express the disdain that powerful nations feel for the rest of the world. The piece combines the attributes of a corporate headquarters, a factory, and a tombstone. It is grease-stained and has computer chip boards tacked to the side, so it looks high tech in some ways. "In God we" is barely visible on the side but "Trust" is big and bold on the bottom of the tombstone.

The Chairman Watching the Game also ties into this theme, referring to the power of multinational corporations and their involvement in regional conflicts, which start out as historical animosities but are then fanned by outsiders with an interest in the outcome. Usually, the sides backed by the local business interests are willing to work with them. But this may not be in the best interest of the people in that country. Here, Stout highlights the war between the Hutus and Tutsis in Rwanda. The piece plays on the notion of the "chairman," sitting up on a chair, high above the action. He is in a light box, because the public does not always know the identities of the real players who call the shots behind some corporate action in another country. On the board, the two black players with the guns pointed at each other are the Hutus and the Tutsis. The white pieces are the "Gang of 8." They just watch. On the bottom of the board, Stout has inscribed in capital letters: "Game rules: For clues to the player's next move, read between the lines of daily paper." On the surface of the glass Stout has silk-screened the objectives for each of the players and the corresponding score if achieved. They include: "Finance Civil War 40 pts.; Encourage Hanging of Dissenters 60 pts.; Destroy Culture 100 pts." Underneath the glass on the board, she has incorporated other images such as battleships, diamonds, part of a $100 bill with Benjamin Franklin's head, and a stamp with Queen Elizabeth's head, as well as extensive text. Model battleships represent the corporate industrial army, because the armies are sometimes designed to protect the interests of these corporations, not citizens. One of the most poignant and visually dramatic elements is the severed head of an African man. A Christian

Opposite page:
The Chairman Watching the Game 1997

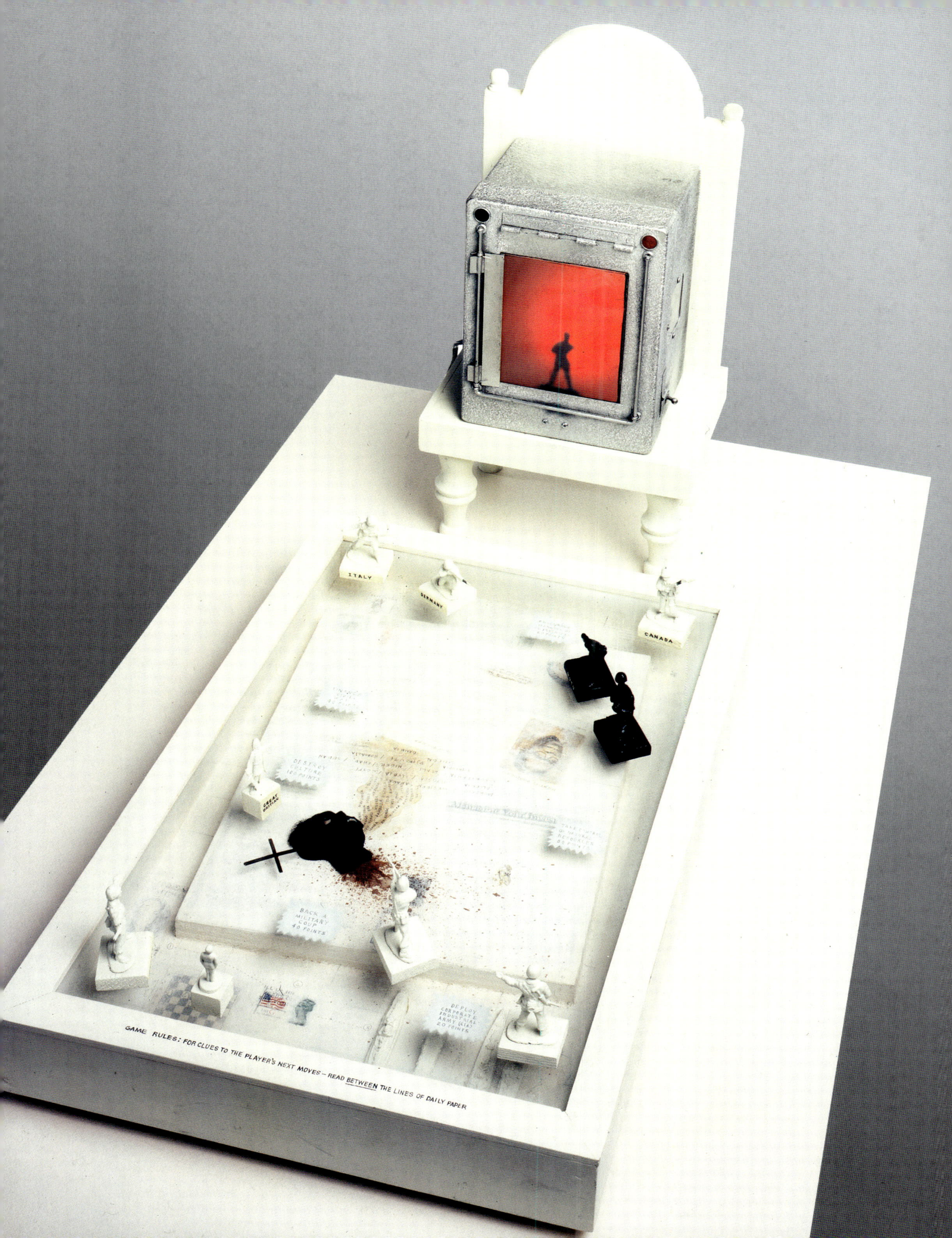
ITALY
GERMANY
CANADA
GREAT BRITIAN
DESTROY CULTURE 100 POINTS
BACK A MILITARY COUP 40 POINTS
GAME RULES: FOR CLUES TO THE PLAYER'S NEXT MOVES – READ BETWEEN THE LINES OF DAILY PAPER

cross is jammed in his ear, and out of his mouth he is spewing all of the native religious traditions that are being replaced by Christianity.

In a series of works focusing on the gun, Stout addresses the need for social change. Not an advocate of violence and dumbfounded that society allows people to own guns, she nevertheless uses the gun as a metaphor for revolution. She finds herself torn: on the one hand, guns are readily available and should not be, but on the other hand, criminals have them, and she herself would like the right to own one for self-defense, not a legal option in D.C.

Although *Point of View* depicts a real gun, Stout invented the guns in her later works. There are nine of them in the series [six in the Belger collection] and they were conceived as a group. The series was inspired by a poetry-reading discussion with several poets describing their emotional state while creating their work. They came to the conclusion that it is very hard to channel emotions into art, because too much gets filtered out. The next morning Stout woke up and decided to wrestle with the question about how to make anger translate into art. She made a gun, because the object was so threatening that it would demand attention. It was Stout's way of holding-up the viewer, jolting him or her into asking why it was there. Stout decided to make guns for people who were revolutionaries trying to change the system, any inequitable system. She made the guns for historical personages such as Harriet Tubman, John Brown, Geronimo, and Che Guevara. None of the guns

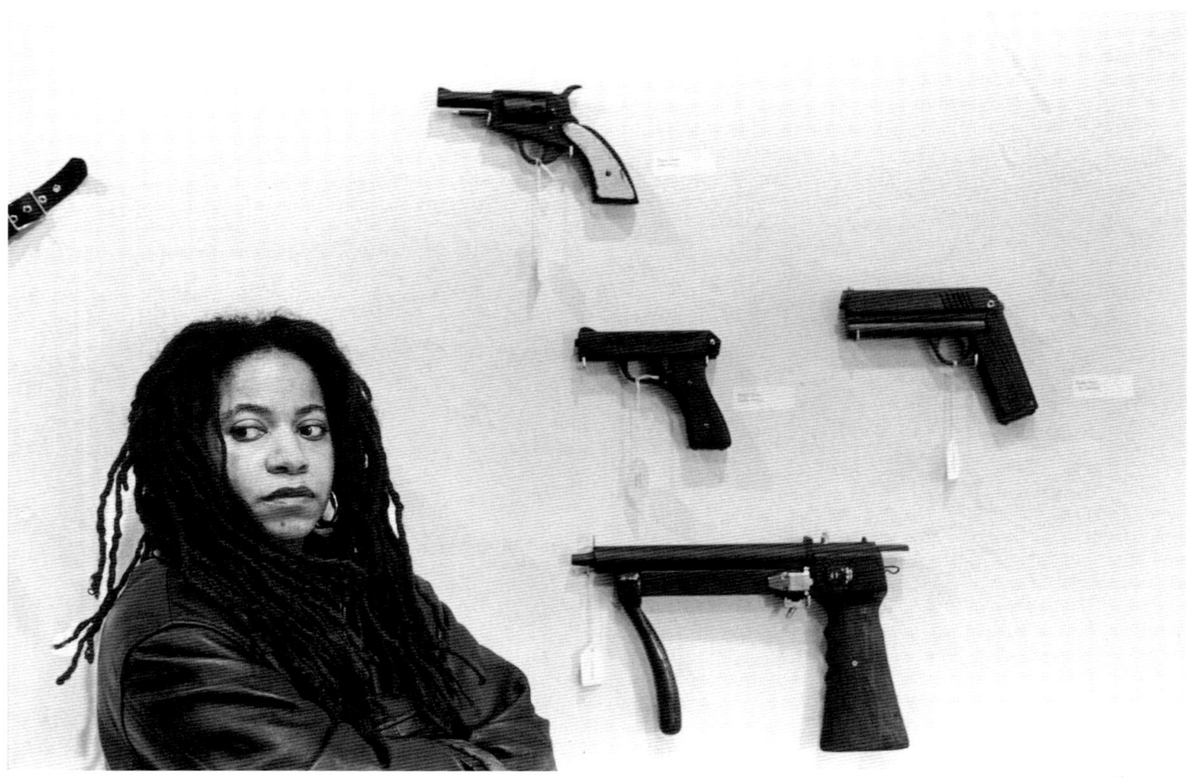

photo by Darrow Montgomery

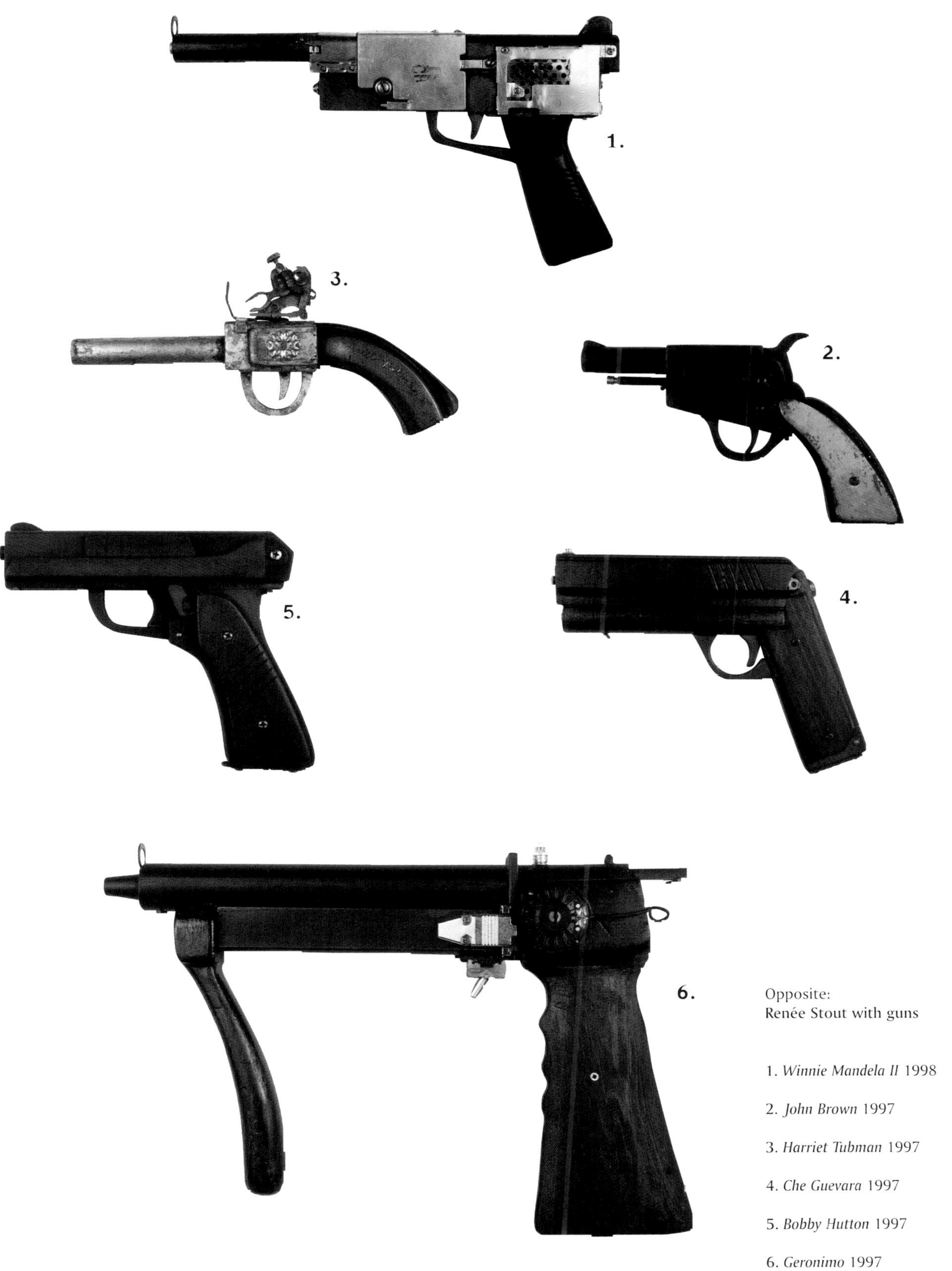

Opposite:
Renée Stout with guns

1. *Winnie Mandela II* 1998

2. *John Brown* 1997

3. *Harriet Tubman* 1997

4. *Che Guevara* 1997

5. *Bobby Hutton* 1997

6. *Geronimo* 1997

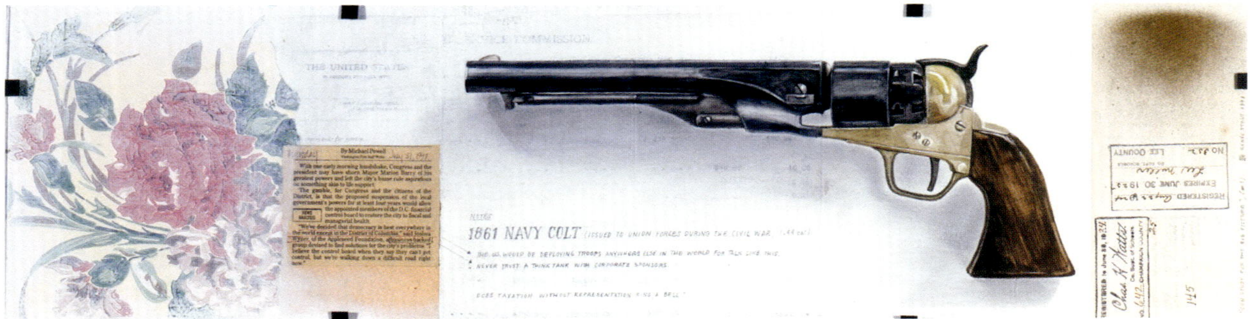

Harriet Carried a Gun Like This 1998

contains any real parts. Instead, each is completely fabricated from wood and metal. Some, like *John Brown*, contain a thread spool for the barrel. Up close, they do not really look like guns, but the whole object reads as a gun, even if the parts do not. In the end, the guns are a metaphor for fighting back, although not a call to arms.

Harriet Carried a Gun Like This displays the same spirit as the revolutionary guns. It was created in the context of the controversy about home rule for the District of Columbia. Someone from a think-tank had made a statement in the press that he believed in freedoms everywhere except in the District. Stout was appalled, so once again she went back to the gun as a metaphor for fighting back. She believes that the Boston Tea Party was about fighting back and asks how anyone can say that certain people in America don't deserve to have freedom. Unlike the guns she created in 1997, *Harriet Carried a Gun Like This* is not a three-dimensional object. Instead, it is a *trompe l'oeil* watercolor of a gun, shown hanging against real wallpaper and text. The effect suggests layers of time and gives it more warmth than the earlier revolutionary guns in their pristine and cool presentation.

Baby's First Gun came later in response to school shootings. Stout observes that adolescent gunmen are tried as adults and made to seem inherently bad, when the real problem is that they do not get the necessary guidance from adults at a point in life when they need it. The piece is called *Baby's First Gun* because American society promotes the idea of the gun as a toy. Stout used a real toy cap gun, but the funny thing is that is has A, B, C on the handle, meaning that it really is designed for a young child. It is resting on a pad covered in yellow and white ticking, like a mattress in a crib. To show its inherent contradictory nature, Stout made a cute-looking baby in a pastel romper with the words, "Society prepares the crime, the criminal commits it," inscribed below. When the box is closed, the top reveals pastel-hued pictures of an elephant and a donkey, for the two political parties, neither of which, Stout believes, has really addressed the issue.

Hustler's Icon addresses the way the music industry promotes and perpetuates a certain kind of greed and competition, so that kids get killed over material possessions such as sports shoes. Inspiration came from watching the kids outside her O Street Studio and recognizing the influence of hip-hop music on them. On one side, Stout affixed a picture of Tupac Shakur and on the other side she put the picture of another rapper, Sean "Puffy" Combs [a.k.a. "P. Diddy"]. In the middle of the piece, Stout again uses symbols from the dollar bill to indicate the greed of the music industry, which makes money by promoting violence among young listeners.

Stout does not consider herself a revolutionary, but she wishes people were more aware of inequities. In her work since 1998 she has continued to press political and social points in combinations of text and imagery, but they have ceased to be the main focus of her art. Her most recent work resonates with her interest in herbal remedies, in pieces that express frustration with the increasingly corporate nature of medicine and its emphasis on profits. Herbal remedies represent the self-empowering idea of turning to nature to stay healthy without having to go through the medical system. In a sense, she has come full circle.

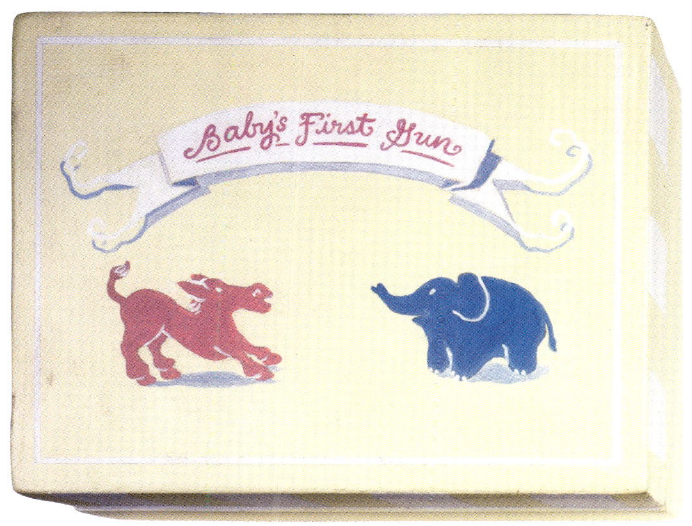

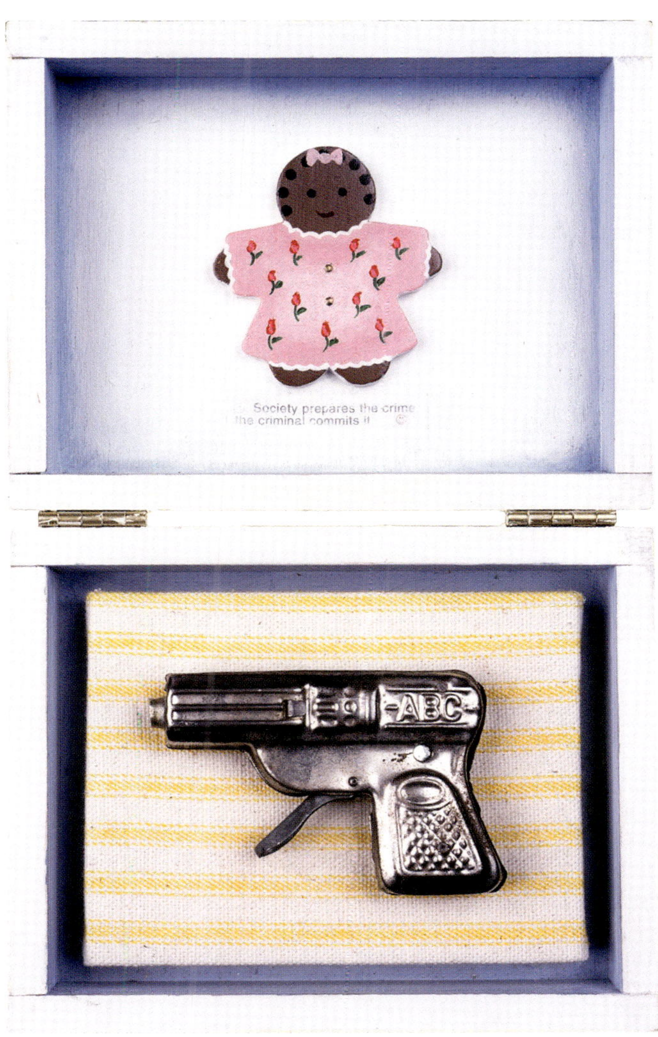

Baby's First Gun 1998
top: box closed
bottom: box open

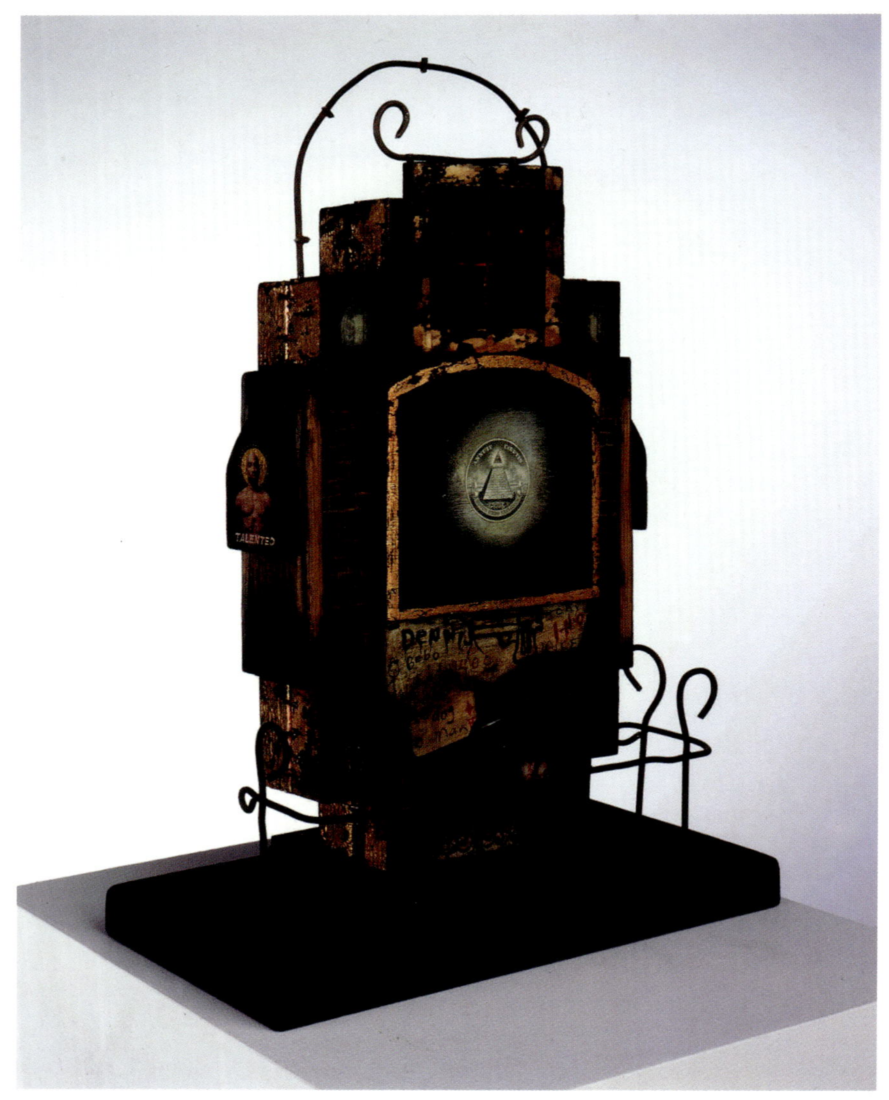

Hustler's Icon 1998

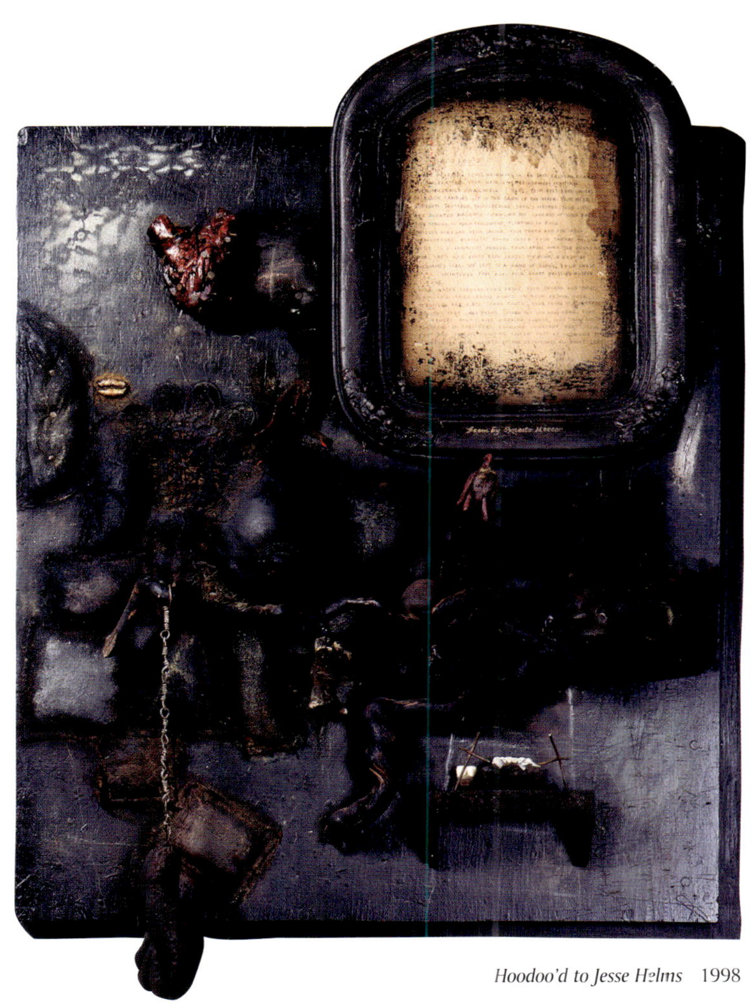

Hoodoo'd to Jesse Helms 1998

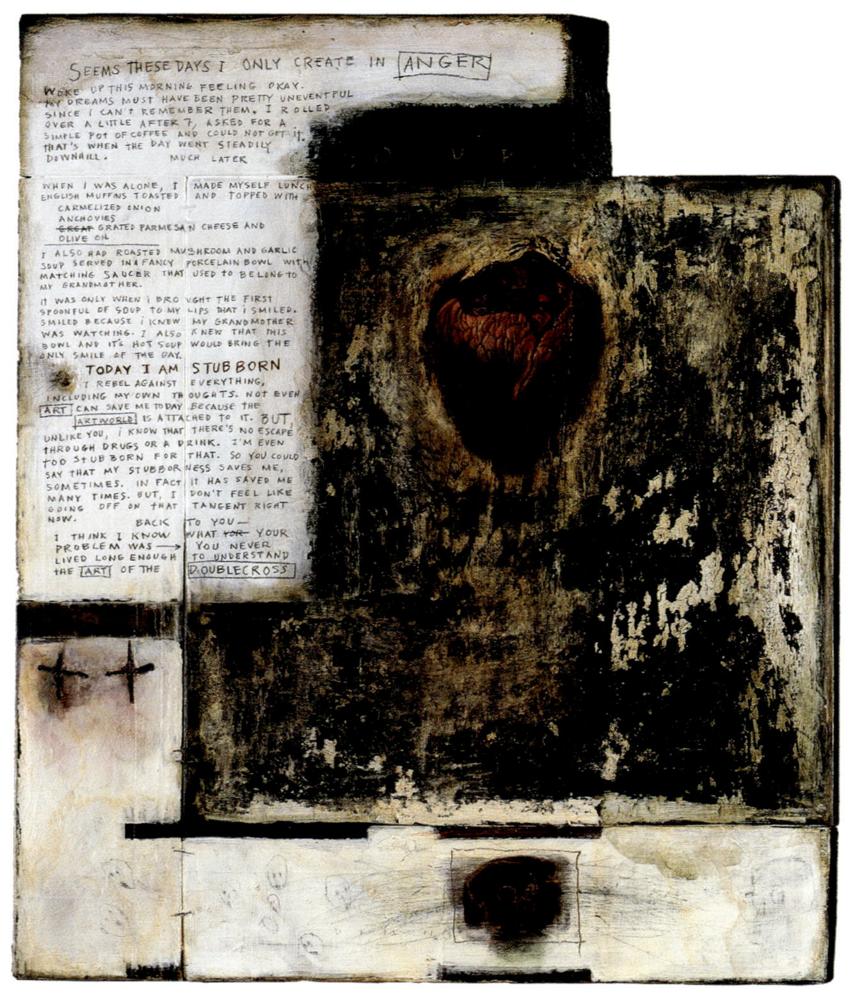

Dancing with Demons 1999

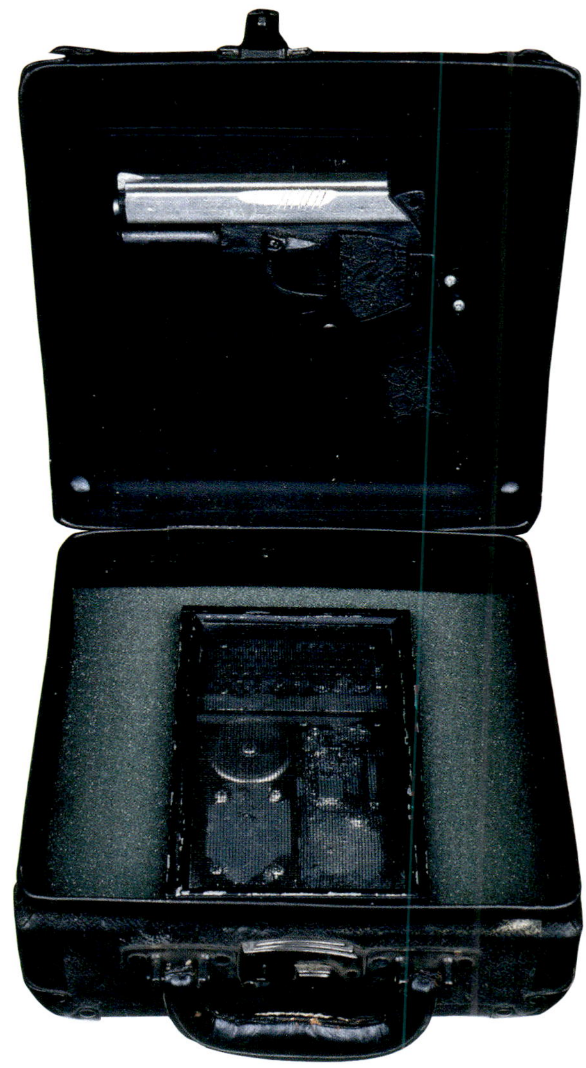

Conspiracy Theory 1998

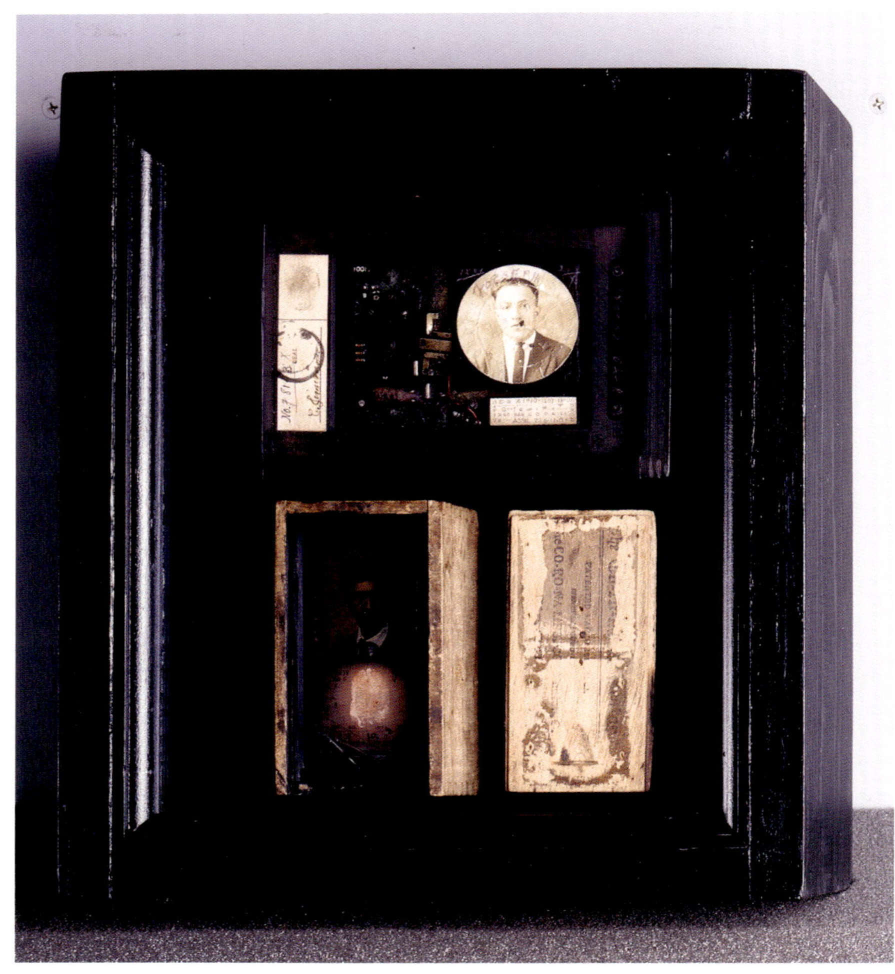

Two Secret Society Passports 1995-96

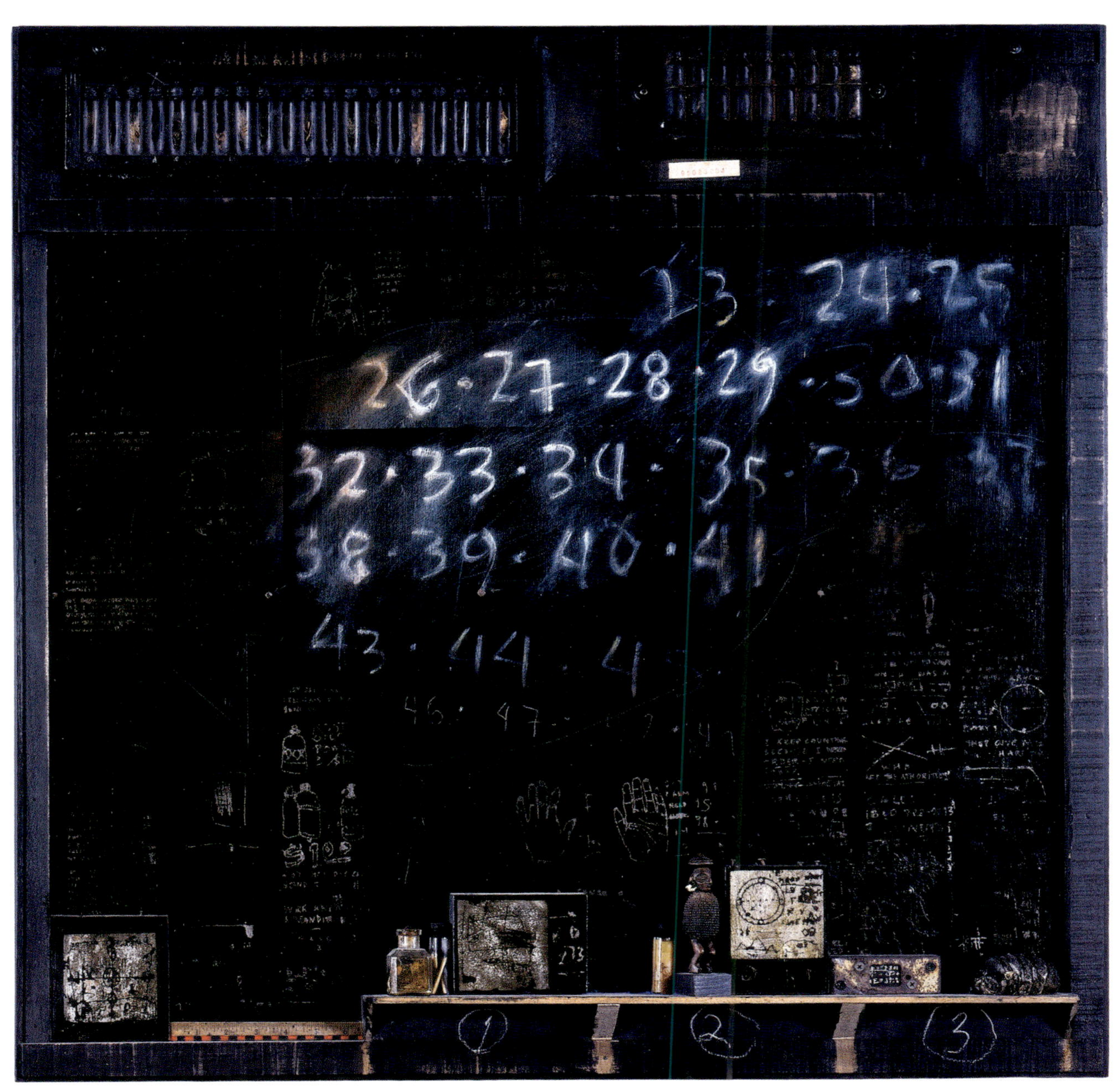

Rarting in the Night Studio 1999

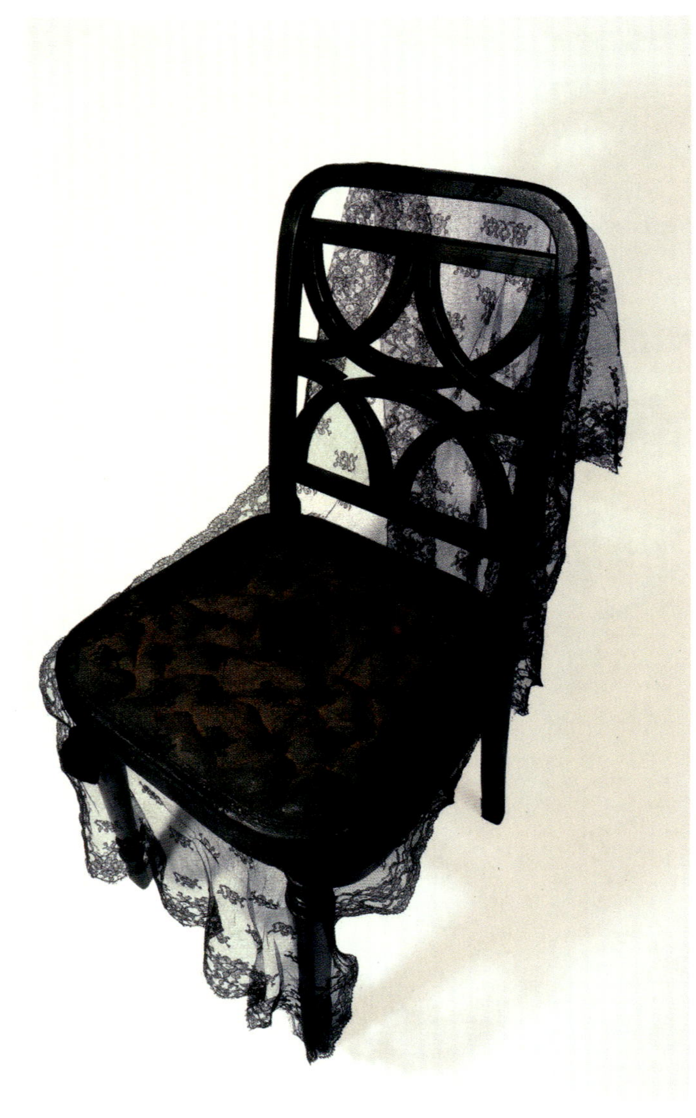

Seat of Power 2001

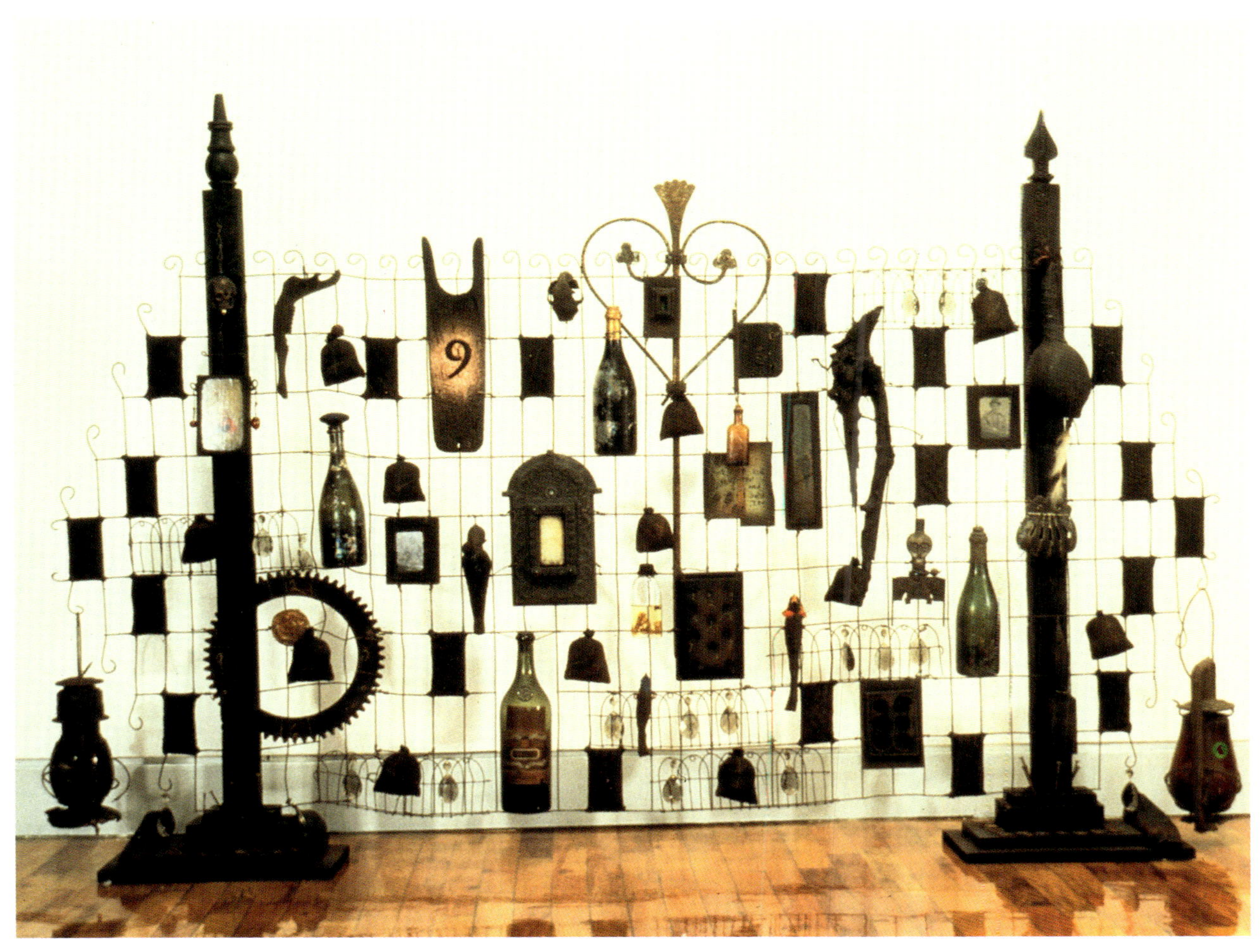

Song of the Cicada 1997

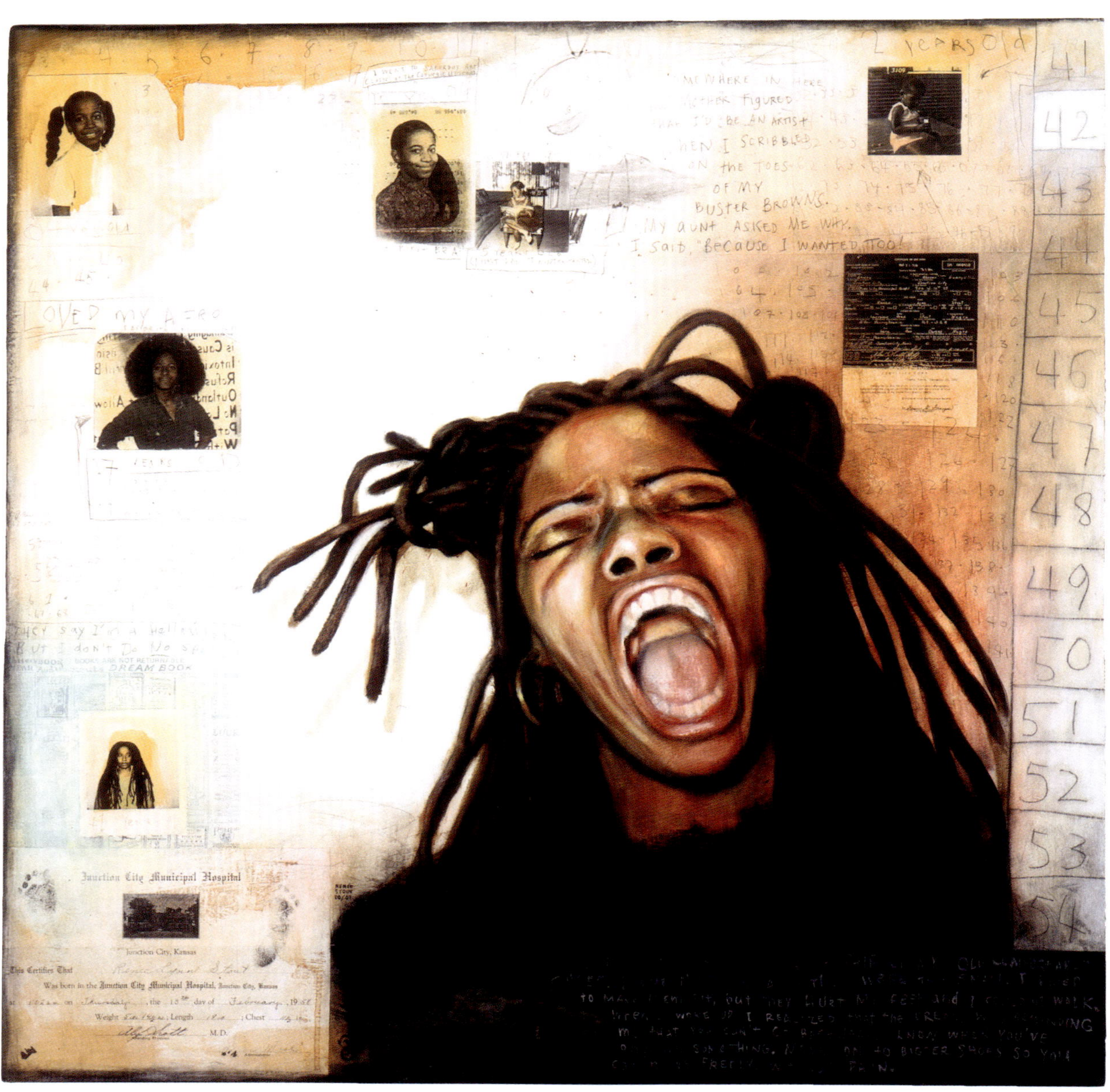
2 years old
figured
BE AN ARTIST
I SCRIBBLED
the TOES
OF MY
BUSTER BROWNS.
My aunt ASKED ME WHY.
I said, "BECAUSE I WANTED TOO!
LOVED MY AFRO
DREAM BOOK
Junction City Municipal Hospital
Junction City, Kansas
This Certifies That
Was born in the Junction City Municipal Hospital
41
42
43
44
45
46
47
48
49
50
51
52
53
54

Transcending Time

Stephen Bennett Phillips and Michelle A. Owen-Workman

Like most art, that of Renée Stout is part imagination and part autobiography. She would like viewers to open their eyes to what may lie beneath the surface, to realize that better understanding comes from opening one's heart and mind to those who have come before and by listening to one's inner spirit. In 1998 she shifted her work's focus to a more private realm. Gone are the overt social and political statements of the preceding two years. Yet, Stout continues to encode her pieces with multiple layers of meaning, both conscious and unconscious. They intersect with an explicit layering of time. While working, she absorbs many tidbits from the world around her, such as song lyrics or news clips on the radio. Unconsciously, she incorporates these fragments into her work, spinning them into creations that speak about her own psyche and individual history. Her embrace of societies that boast strong spiritual traditions has helped to create an iconography that is both personal and universal.

Religion continues to play a large role in Stout's work, although she does not subscribe to any particular faith. To her, all religions have an interesting philosophical viewpoint and they all have the same spiritual goal of connecting people with a higher power. Stout tries to extract the positive elements from each religion and to ignore the negative. Her series on storefront church architecture addresses her amalgam of Baptist church and Vodou practices. In many ways, some African religious beliefs remain unspoken among African Americans. Stout's paternal grandmother does not accept her current work because of its strong Vodou connotations. Stout has discovered many devout Christians ordering herbs and requesting spiritual guidance from root-workers. Most would not want members of their church to know they frequented "root stores."

Since Vodou went underground in the 1920s, African-Americans have been reluctant to discuss it, even at home. Recently, Stout's mother sent her a small article about a relative who is known as a healer in the community. The article devoted considerable space to her work as a Christian volunteer but ignored her "healing" activities. After many years of probing by her daughter, Stout's mother has finally revealed stories of spiritual healers within the family. Around 1996 Stout discovered the name of a second cousin in *A Company of Prophets*, a book about seers. Although fascinated with the discovery of secret healers within her family, she is reluctant to ask too many questions.

Venturing out on her own, she searches for answers and ponders the connections between Christianity and Vodou. Stout discovers visual clues in the many storefront churches around Washington, D.C. These churches are often converted retail spaces or houses located in African-American neighborhoods. With her camera, she documents their vanishing facades. Her artwork records a unique vernacular architecture that is slowly being

Opposite page:
Scream at 42 2001

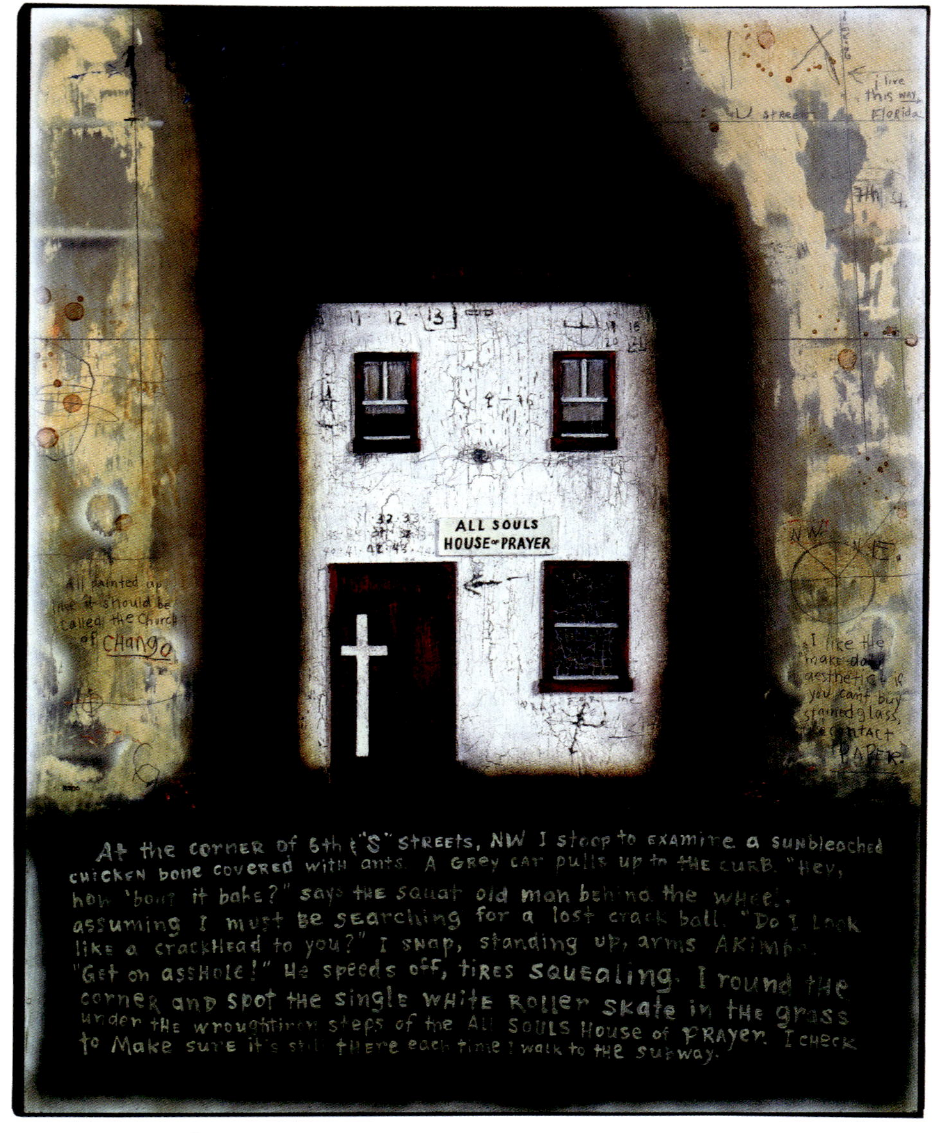

The All Souls House of Prayer 2000

lost to gentrification. According to Stout, they have an aesthetic quality that exudes spontaneity. With a sense of immediacy and determination, their exterior design screams, "Look at us. We have something to say." They also allude to the integration of African-based religions with Christianity.

The All Souls House of Prayer states it is "all painted up like it should be called the church of Chango." While the church is Baptist, Chango is derived from a West African deity represented by the colors red and white. In the *Sign from Grandma Bea's Church*, the figure of Jesus is removed from his traditional cross and replaced with a red cross that is similar to a Kongo cosmogram or a Yoruba crossroads. The sign's decorative wooden embellishment is remarkably similar to Haitian veve.

Stout loves to personify objects within interior spaces. During the early 1980s, when she was still living in Pittsburgh, she scavenged through abandoned houses in the city's Hill District. At the time, she didn't understand why she responded to them, as she walked through and studied the patterns of peeling wallpaper, old flaking paint, warped floor boards, cracked linoleum, and shreds of polyester lace curtains still hanging on the windows. Later, she came to realize that the decaying interiors echoed her sense of melancholy, which she expressed by drawing the viewer into the intimate space of the pieces with a seductively welcoming combination of colors and shapes. Once the viewer has entered the space, the interior details become disconcerting. The initial feeling of well-being changes to disquiet. Details such as bones, teeth, snakes, and vivid short stories cut against the beautiful facade. Stout equates this reaction with the start of a new relationship. Appearances are not always what they appear to be on the surface or from a distance. Closer inspection of *The Lovers* shows that a beautiful white lace cushion adorned with delicate pink roses is actually two dead parakeets intricately wrapped in individual beaded casings.

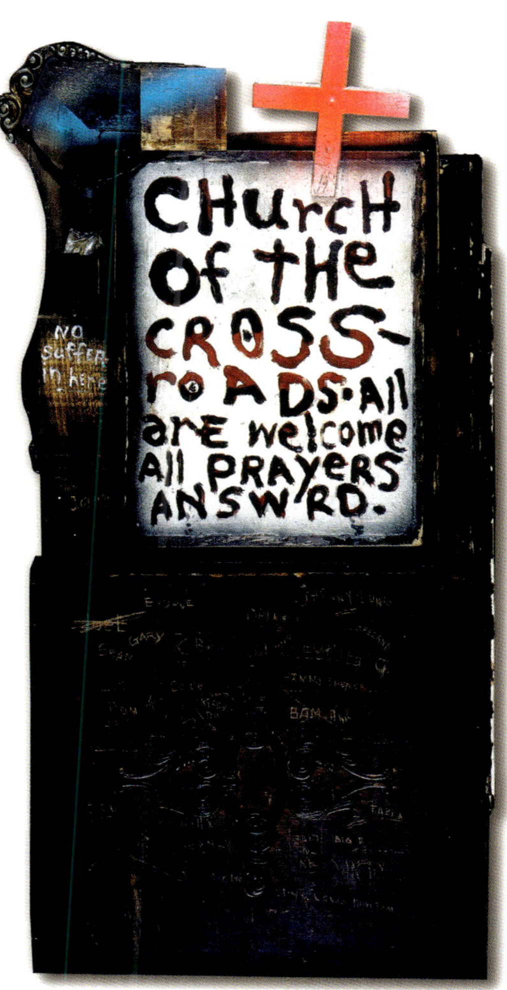

Sign from Granama Bea's Church 1997

In 1999 Stout purchased her first house, which she also uses as a studio. Similar to the old abandoned ones she used to explore in Pittsburgh, her ninety-nine-year-old house has seen numerous owners and residents. Stout believes that interior spaces have a life of their own, a "spirit" of sorts, which is created over time by the people who have lived within their walls. With each living presence a new facet of the "spirit" comes into being. Stout is interested in chipping away at the exterior layer in order to reveal all of the layers beneath the surface. In *Storefront Church* (p. III) Stout produces a cross-section of all the layers of time within a single picture, so that past and present appear simultaneously. Although her collages may look like a fragmented collection of odds and ends, they are, in fact, a cohesive combination of the significant details of one space traced through time.

Gender and relationship issues continue to shape Stout's work. Her series on love charms examines the obsession with love and its fantastical connotations. In her recent work, she makes objects such as love potions and lucky gambler kits that address the desire for happiness, particularly in love, and financial prosperity. Stout herself is a happy person, but looking at society, she sees people constantly trying to improve their financial situation. They live hard lives and, needing money, they play

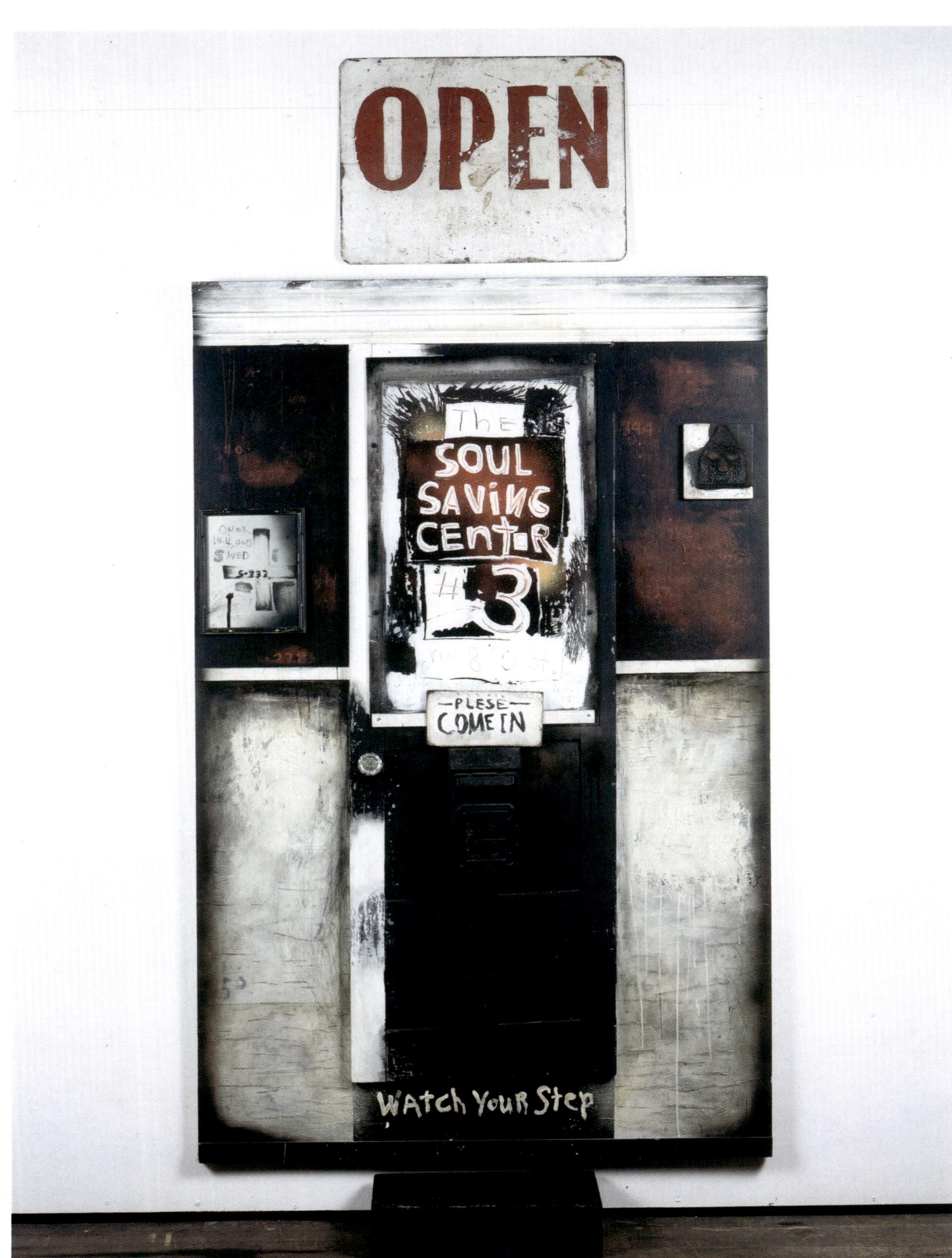
OPEN
The
SOUL
SAVING
CENTOR
#3
PLESE
COME IN
OVER
144,000
SAVED
Watch Your Step

the lottery. Growing up, she herself did not witness a trusting intimate relationship between her parents or her grandparents. Stout remembers friction in her own parents' relationship and the sense of uncertainty it caused her. Her parents divorced when Stout was in her thirties, having stayed together for the sake of their children. Their unhappiness affected Stout's views on marriage. She does not fully trust love relationships and continues to struggle with these issues in her life and in her art. Before her own relationship broke up, Stout started to work on *Scream at 42* (p.63) to commemorate her forty-second birthday. The piece includes numbers and photographs of herself as a child and adolescent. As she worked she sensed that things were a little strange with her lover, so she put the painting aside for a while and started working on other pieces. In hindsight she thinks that she painted herself screaming, perhaps, because at some level she was aware of the disintegration of the relationship. She was unable to go on with the painting until three months after the breakup. Only then could she recognize the feelings behind the scream.

The fictional character of Fatima Mayfield emerged during the breakup of this relationship. Stout creates alter egos to personify coveted characteristics and as a means to work through issues of personal growth. In essence, Fatima is the woman the artist aspires to be. However, she is not just a facet of Stout's personality but represents all women who rise up to face adversity. Fatima personifies the hidden strength of women and dispels societal constraints on them. She is roughly based on the Yoruba goddess, Oya, the patron of feminine leadership, fundamental knowledge, and eternal change. Stout extracted Oya's characteristics from the many strong women who have influenced her life, including her mother, her grandmother, and even the crack-head woman called Poochie, who hung around outside Stout's former residence on O Street. Fatima is a metaphor for self-discovery and self-empowerment just like another alter ego, Madam Ching. But there's nothing "polite" about Fatima. She is younger and more brazen, because Stout's view on womanhood has changed over time. When she was younger, she was shy about expressing her feelings. As she sees it, only older people openly express their feelings. As though empowered by Fatima, Stout has grown stronger and now is more than willing to speak her mind.

Stout is fascinated by the realization that humans occupy only one small part of time and space. Previous generations move in and out of the current mortal realm. People can acknowledge their presence and communicate with them, or they can ignore them and go about their daily lives. This fusion of generations can be seen through the eyes of her multiple alter egos, like Fatima. These characters remain in contact with earlier generations, seek their advice, and devote themselves to a life of healing and conjuration. Dorothy and Col. Frank were Stout's first two alter egos. They grew from Stout's desire to understand both the female and male point of view within a relationship. *She Kept Her Conjuring Table Very Neat* depicts a secret conjuring table used by Dorothy to manipulate the dynamics of her relationship with Col. Frank.

Opposite page:
Soul Saving Center #3 1998

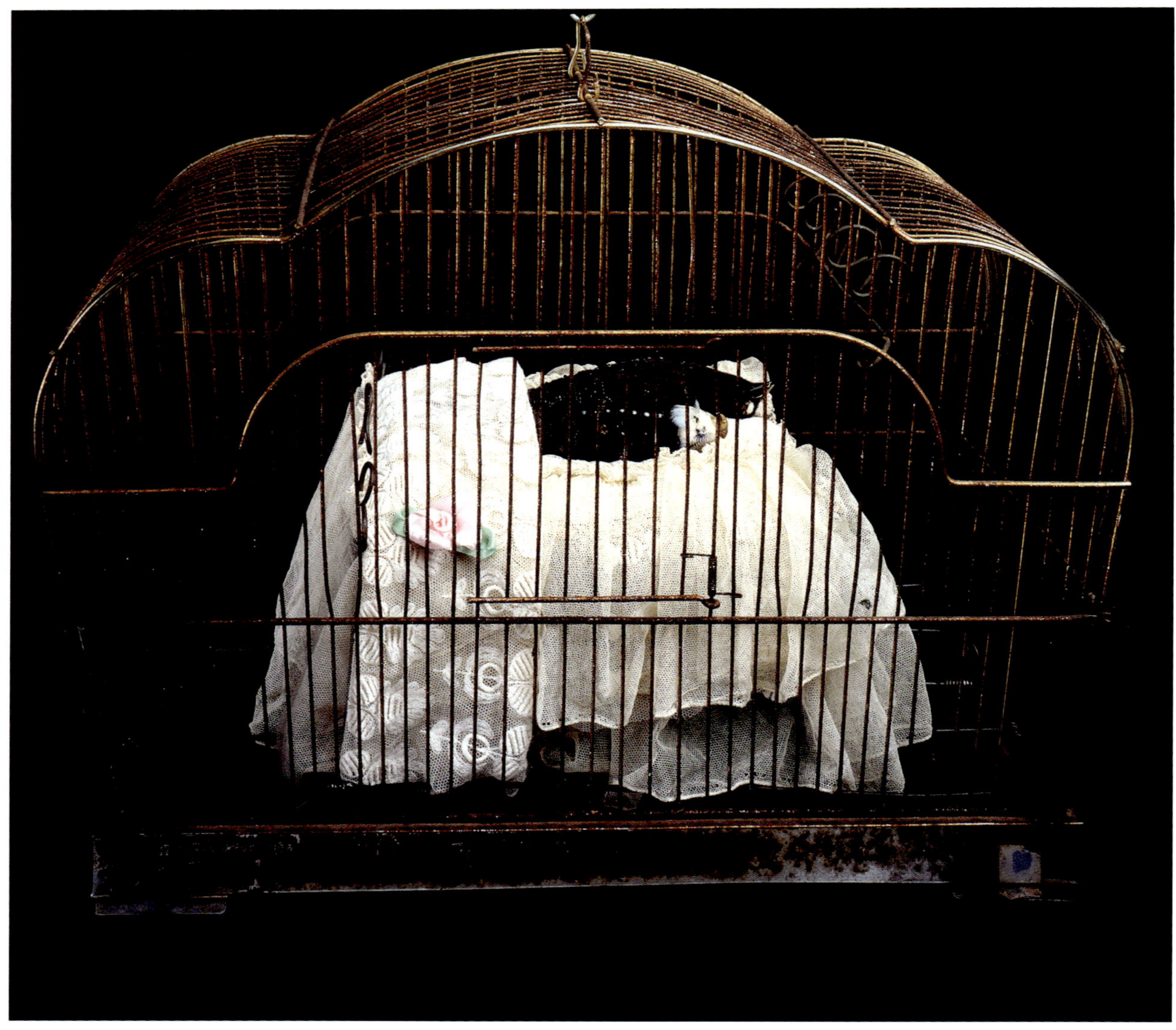

The Lovers 1998

Madam Ching emerged in 1992 and inhabited Stout's art until around 1996. Two years later, Fatima and her love interest, Sterling Rochambeau, took Madam Ching's place. Fatima is a middle-aged African-American woman who inherited her aunt's root store filled with decades' worth of potions, roots, and advertisements. Fatima knows what some of the items are, but others remain a total mystery. The works of art that arise out of this fiction purport to be time-worn items from the store. Their appearance has changed over the decades: an old ad for a love potion has a layer of grime on the surface, the bottle itself is partially covered with dust, and the background sign reveals random notes added over time by Fatima's aunt, as well as a telephone number belonging to a former customer and a scribbled potion. All these elements bear witness to the past. Some of the objects are numbered, but the key to these numbers is long lost.

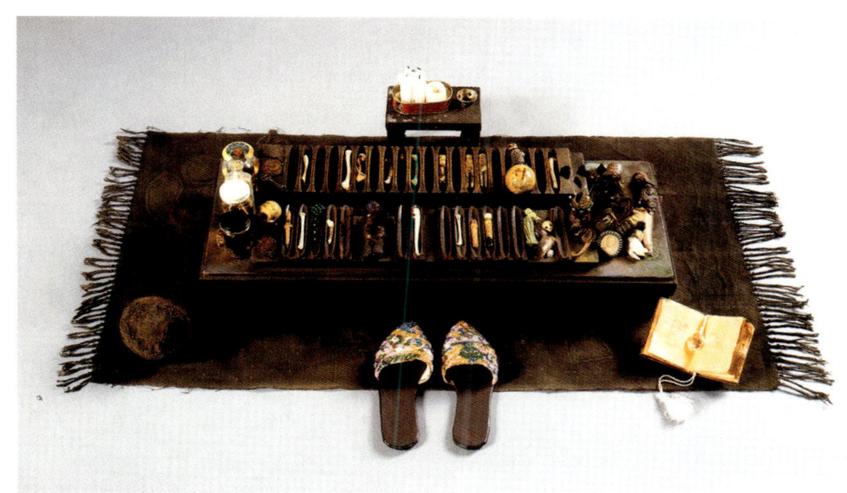

She Kept Her Conjuring Table Very Neat 1992

Fatima inherited the root store because Stout wants to preserve these root stores. So much is lost when the older generation dies. Viewers are initiated into the world of Fatima Mayfield through the numerous advertisements promoting the herbal remedies sold in Fatima's root store. They recall Stout's apprenticeship with a sign painter shortly after college. She is drawn to a variety of signs, but especially those with neon and amateur graphics. She also loves folk signs with their misspelled words and uneven lettering. *Fatima's Sign* is Stout's tribute to folk signs with handwritten text laboriously printed on the oversized storefront sign. Stout hopes to write a book about Fatima Mayfield, but for now her prose is limited to the texts attached to the pieces, written words that summon spirits and offer the viewer fragments of the fiction that underlies her art.

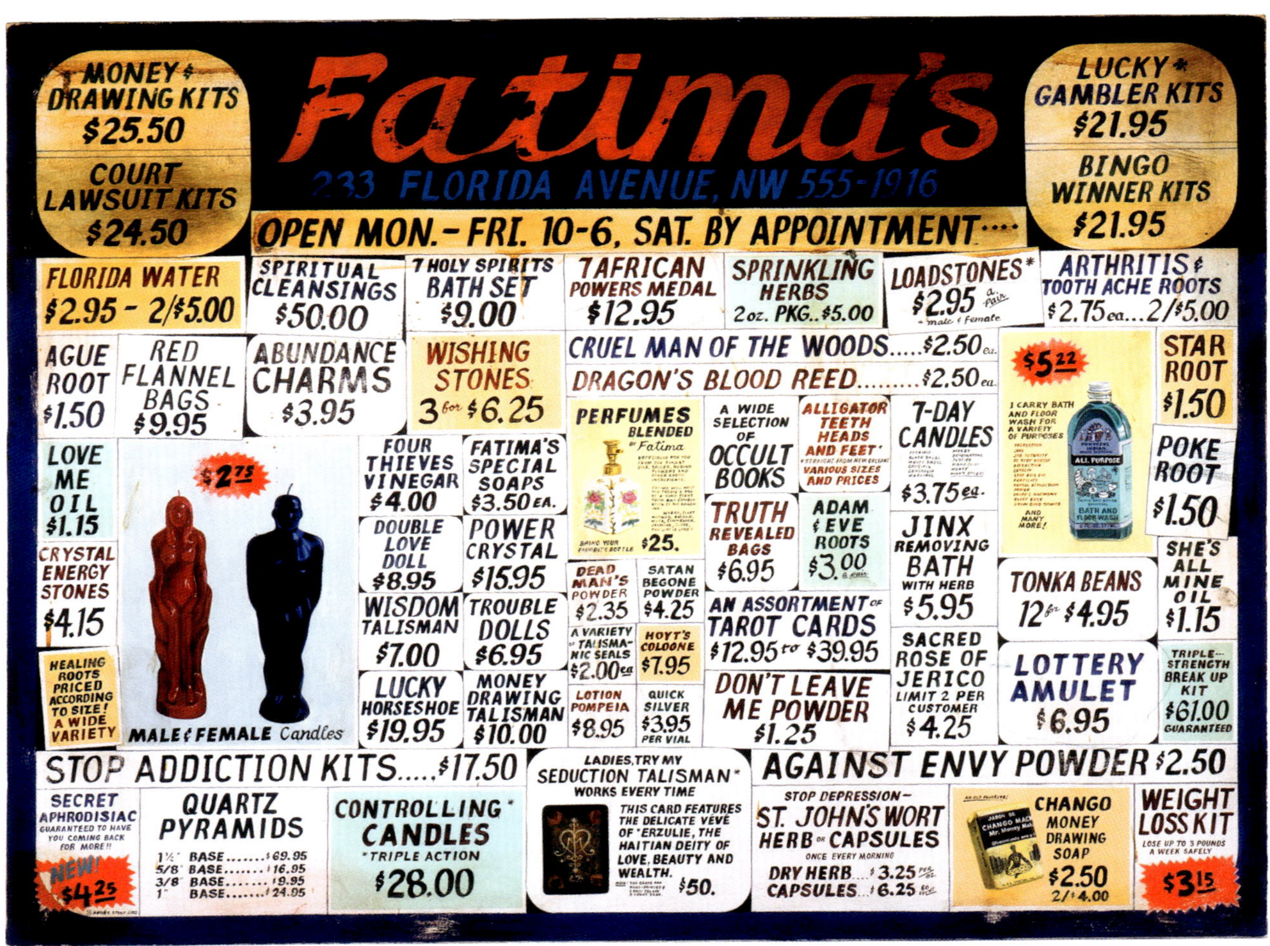

Fatima's Sign 2001

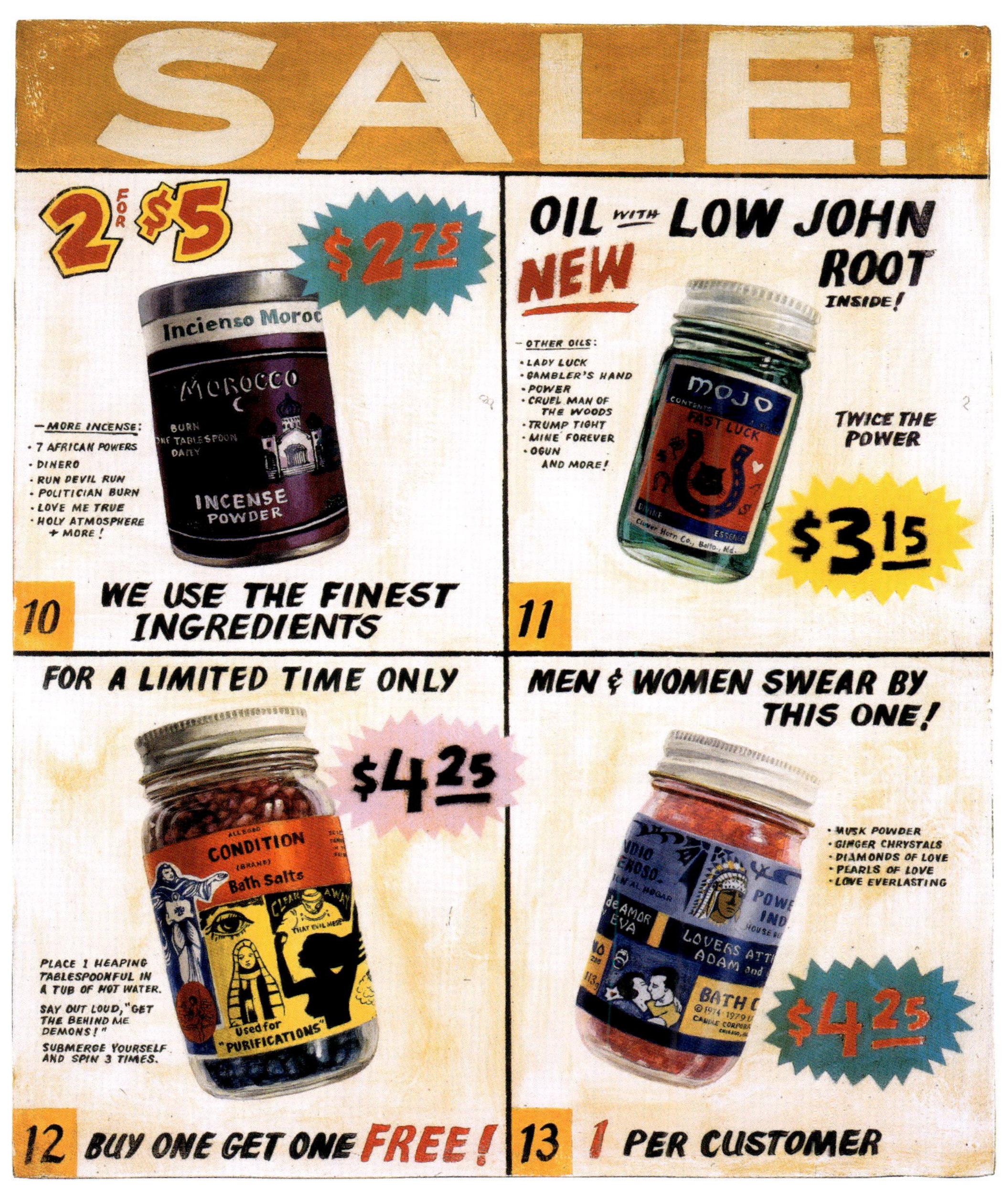

Two for Five 2002

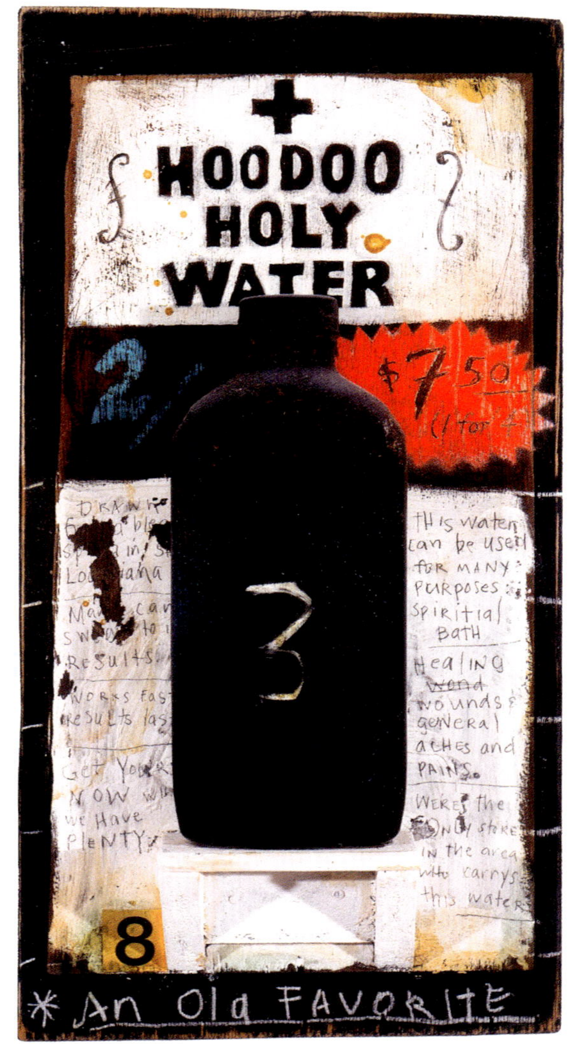

Hoodoo Holy Water 2001

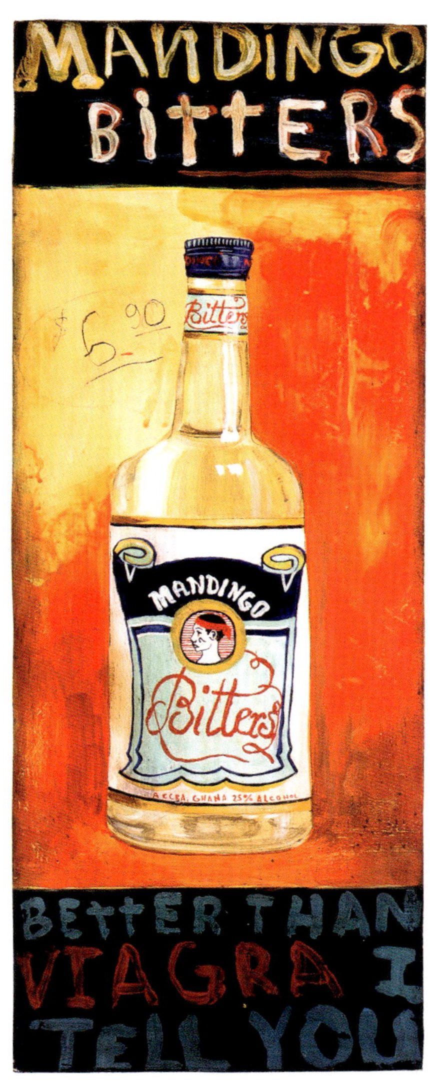

Mandingo Bitters 2002

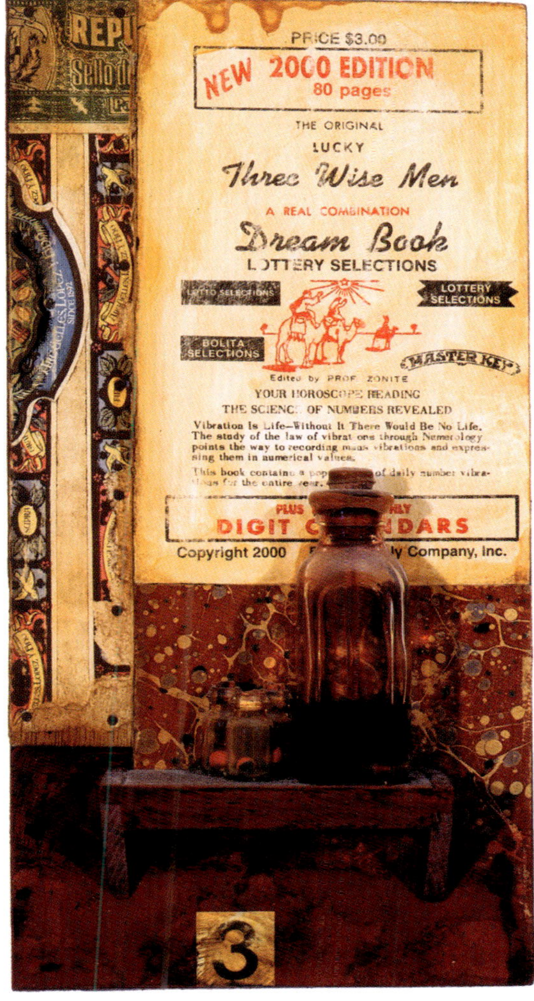

Three Wise Men 2001

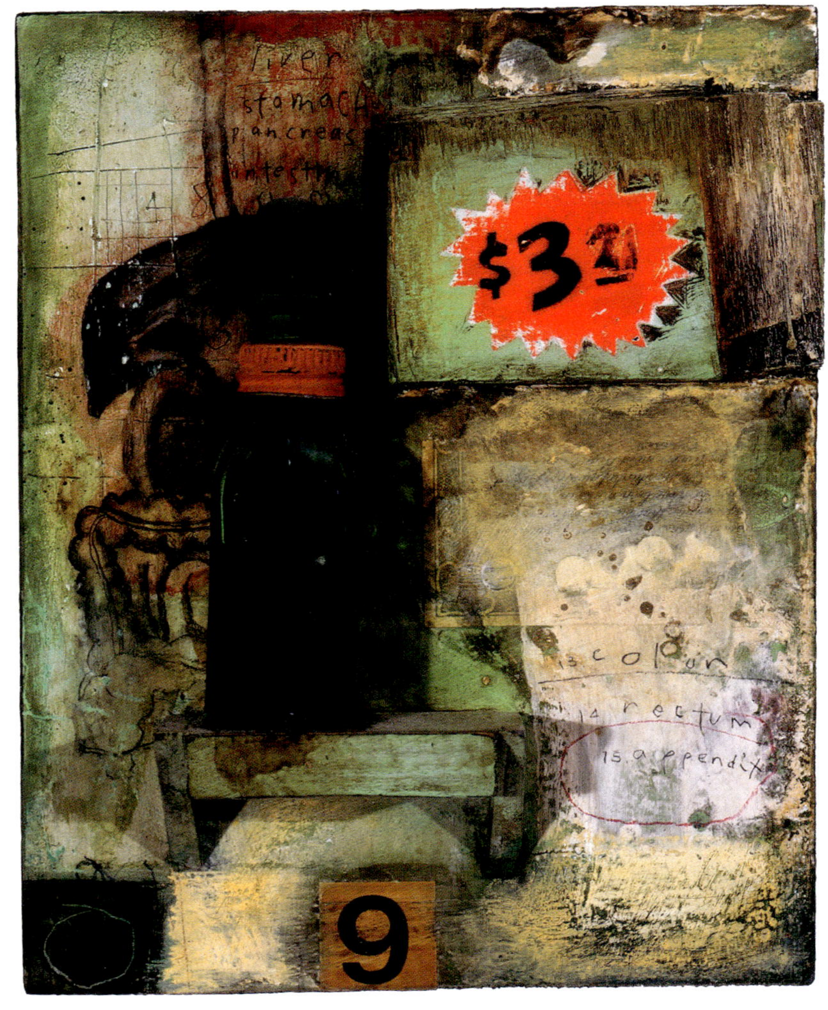

Liver, Stomach, Pancreas 2001

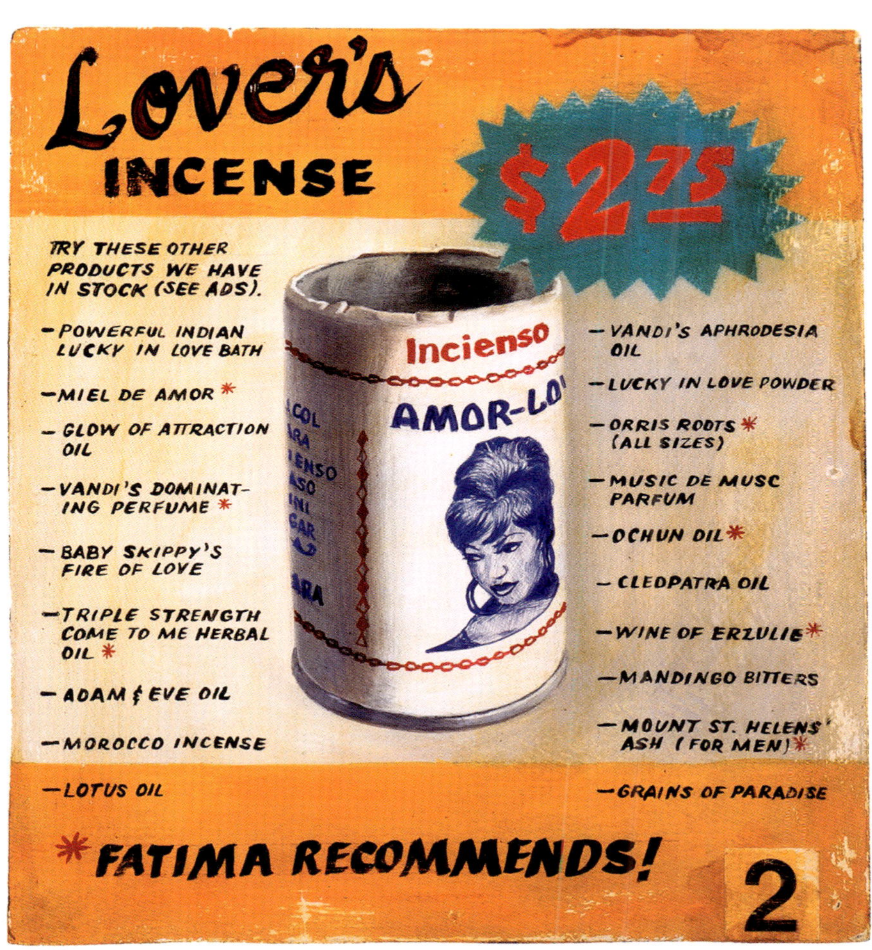
Lover's
INCENSE
$2.75
TRY THESE OTHER PRODUCTS WE HAVE IN STOCK (SEE ADS).
—POWERFUL INDIAN LUCKY IN LOVE BATH
—MIEL DE AMOR *
—GLOW OF ATTRACTION OIL
—VANDI'S DOMINATING PERFUME *
—BABY SKIPPY'S FIRE OF LOVE
—TRIPLE STRENGTH COME TO ME HERBAL OIL *
—ADAM & EVE OIL
—MOROCCO INCENSE
—LOTUS OIL
Incienso
AMOR-LO
—VANDI'S APHRODESIA OIL
—LUCKY IN LOVE POWDER
—ORRIS ROOTS * (ALL SIZES)
—MUSIC DE MUSC PARFUM
—OCHUN OIL *
—CLEOPATRA OIL
—WINE OF ERZULIE *
—MANDINGO BITTERS
—MOUNT ST. HELENS' ASH (FOR MEN) *
—GRAINS OF PARADISE
* FATIMA RECOMMENDS!
2

Amor II 2001

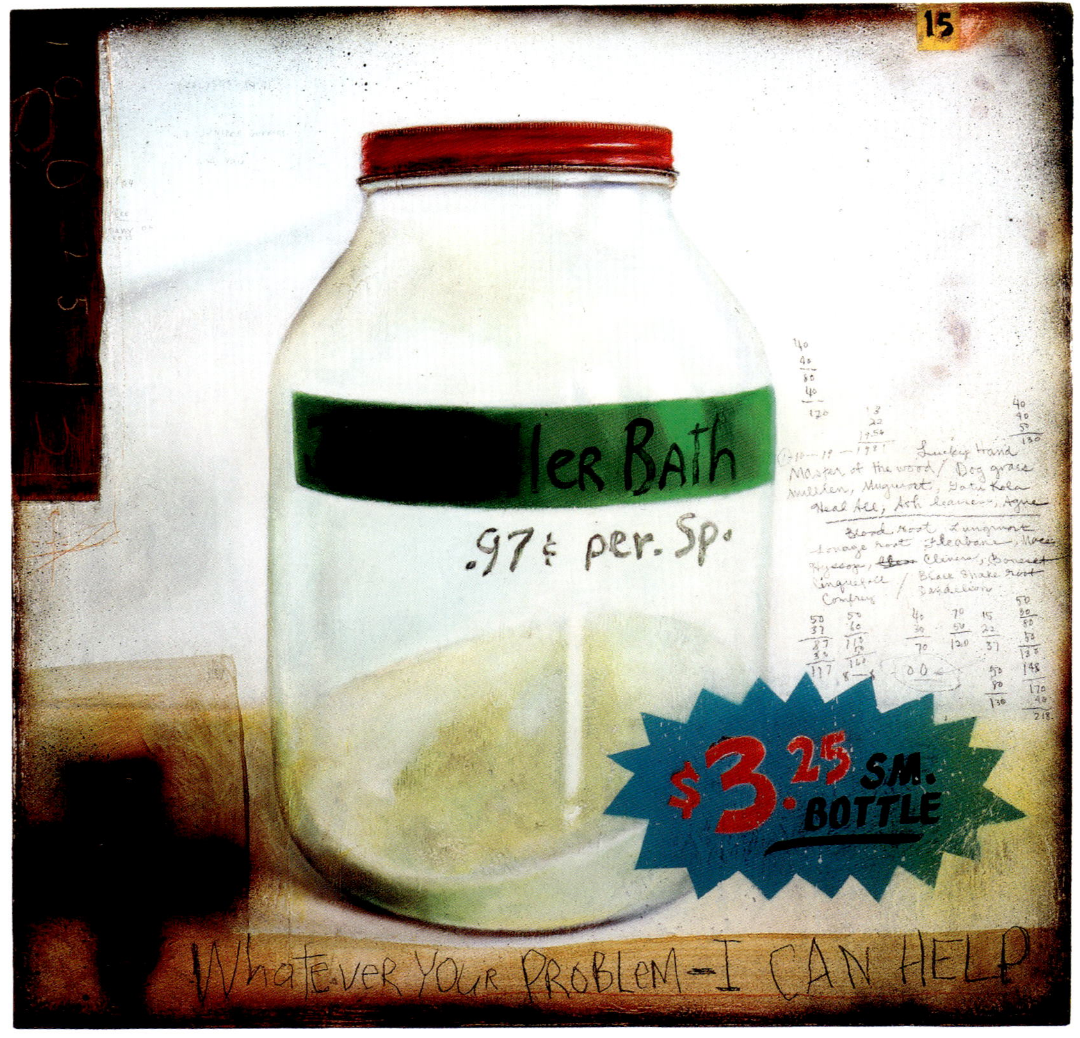

Jinx Killer Bath 2002

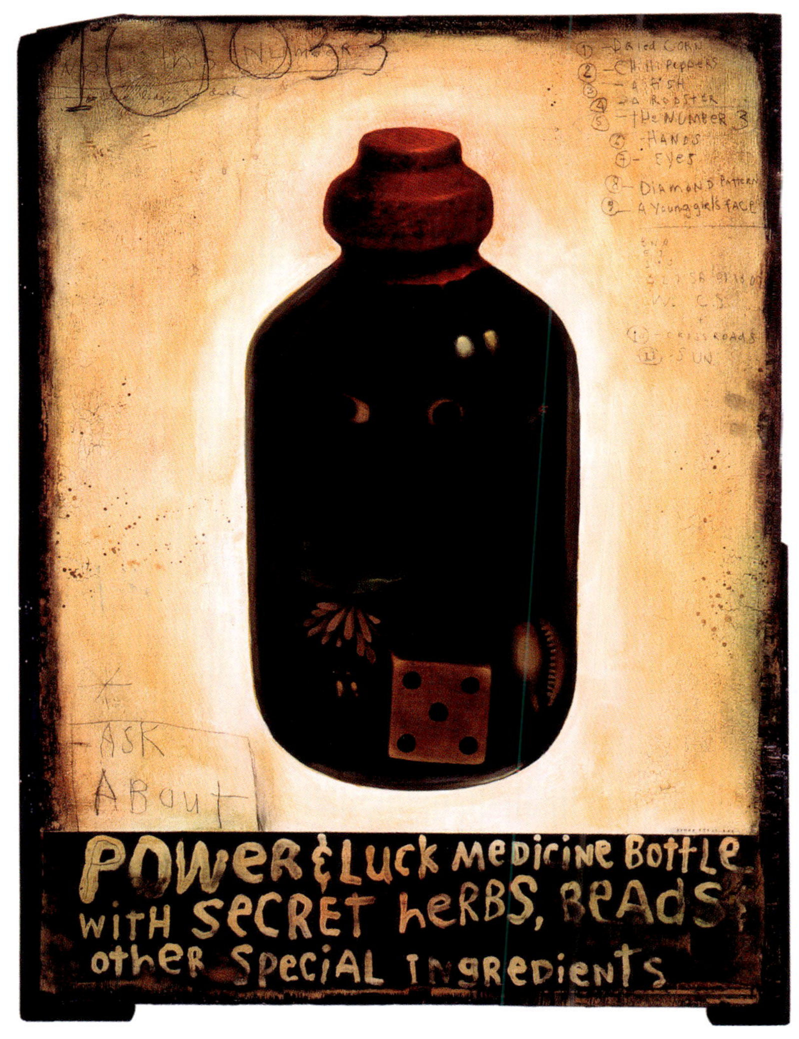

Power and Luck 2002

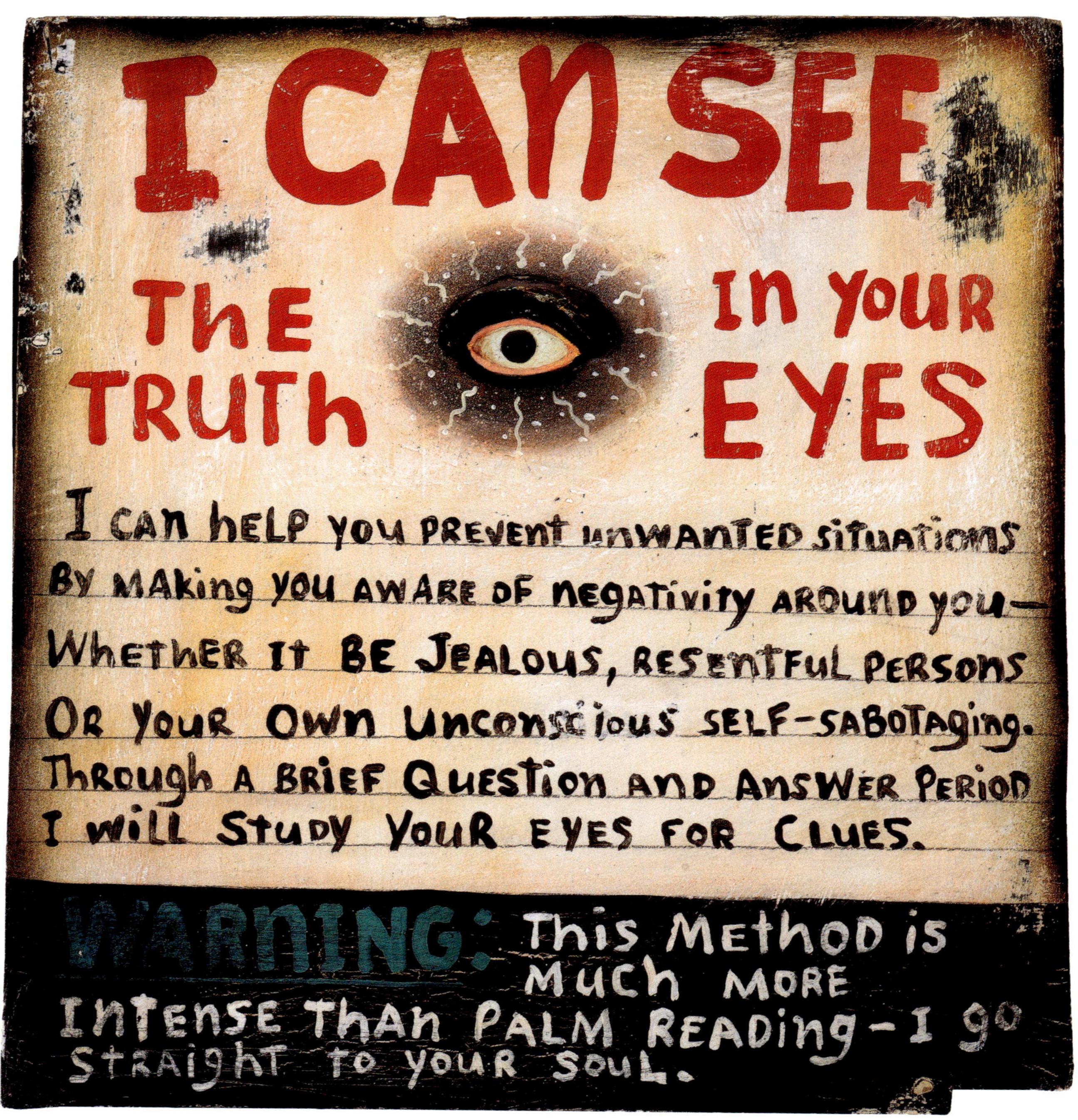

See the Truth 2001

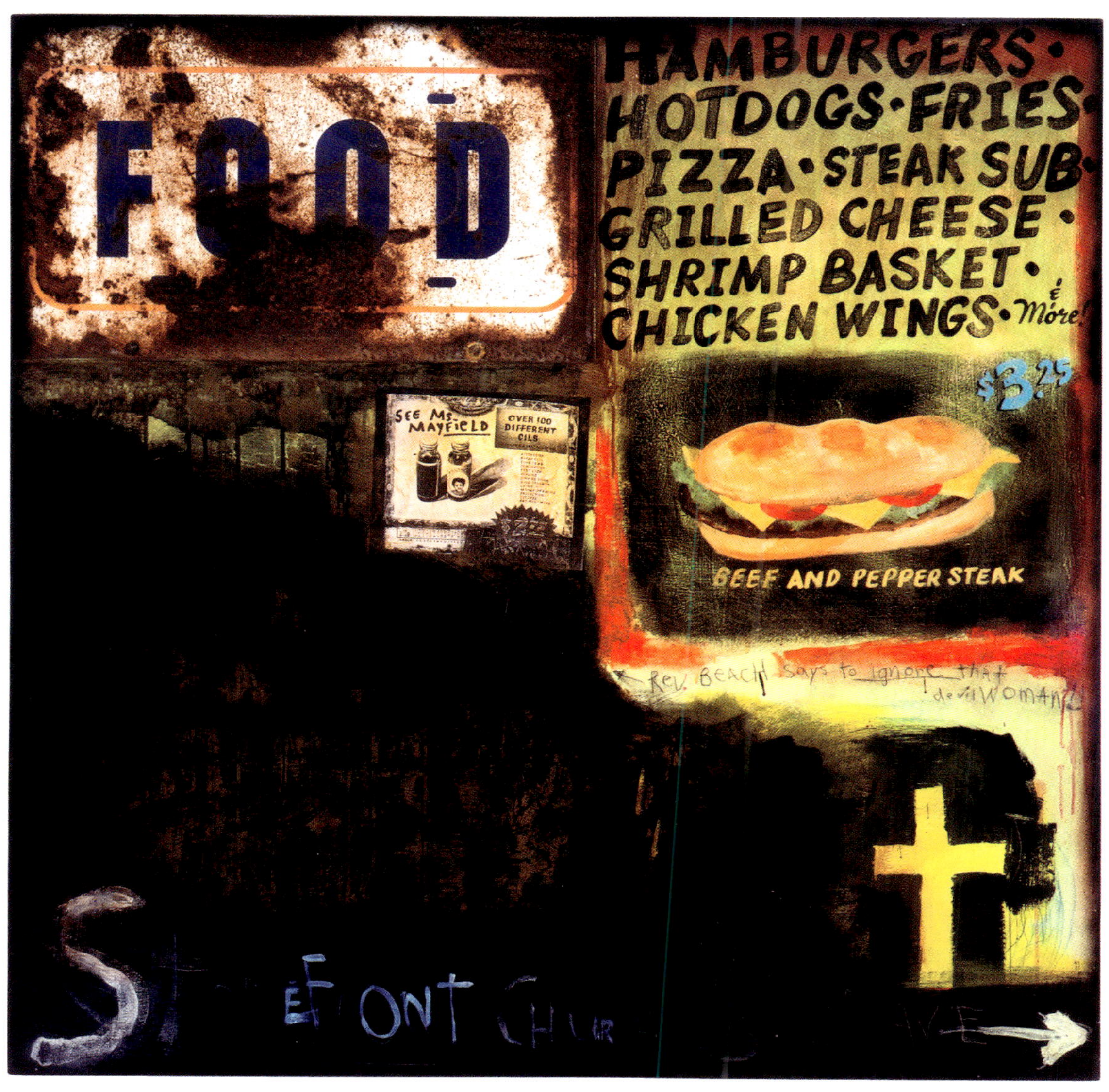

Storefront Church Georgia Avenue 2000

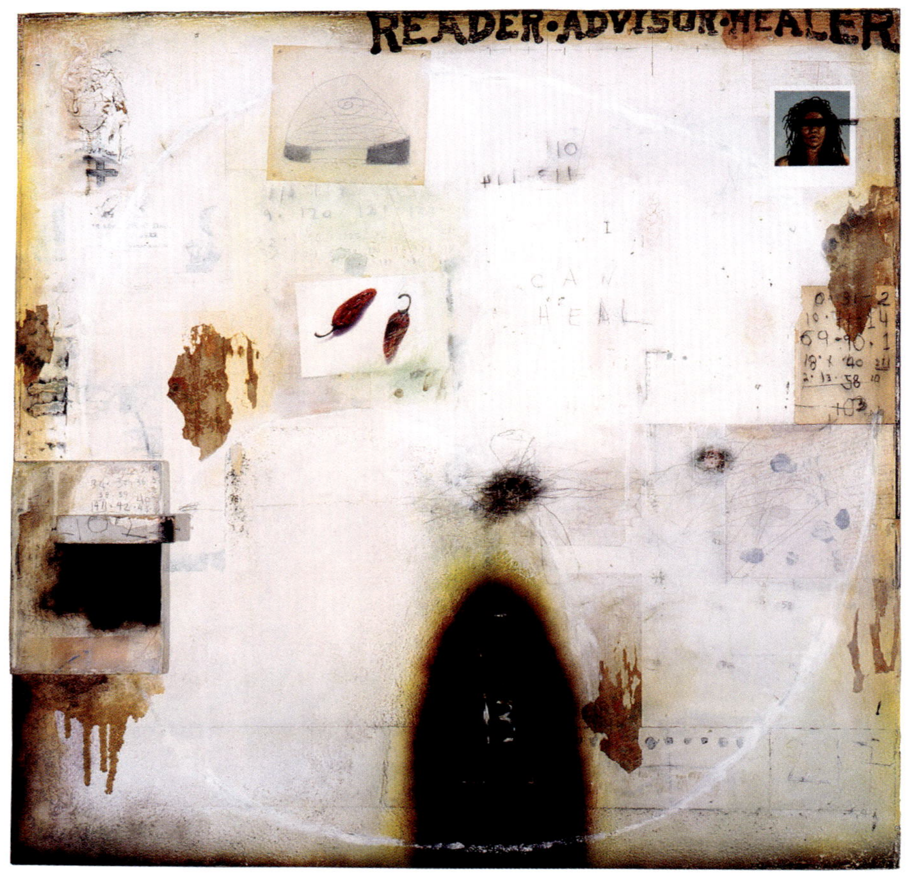

Healer, Heal Thyself 2000

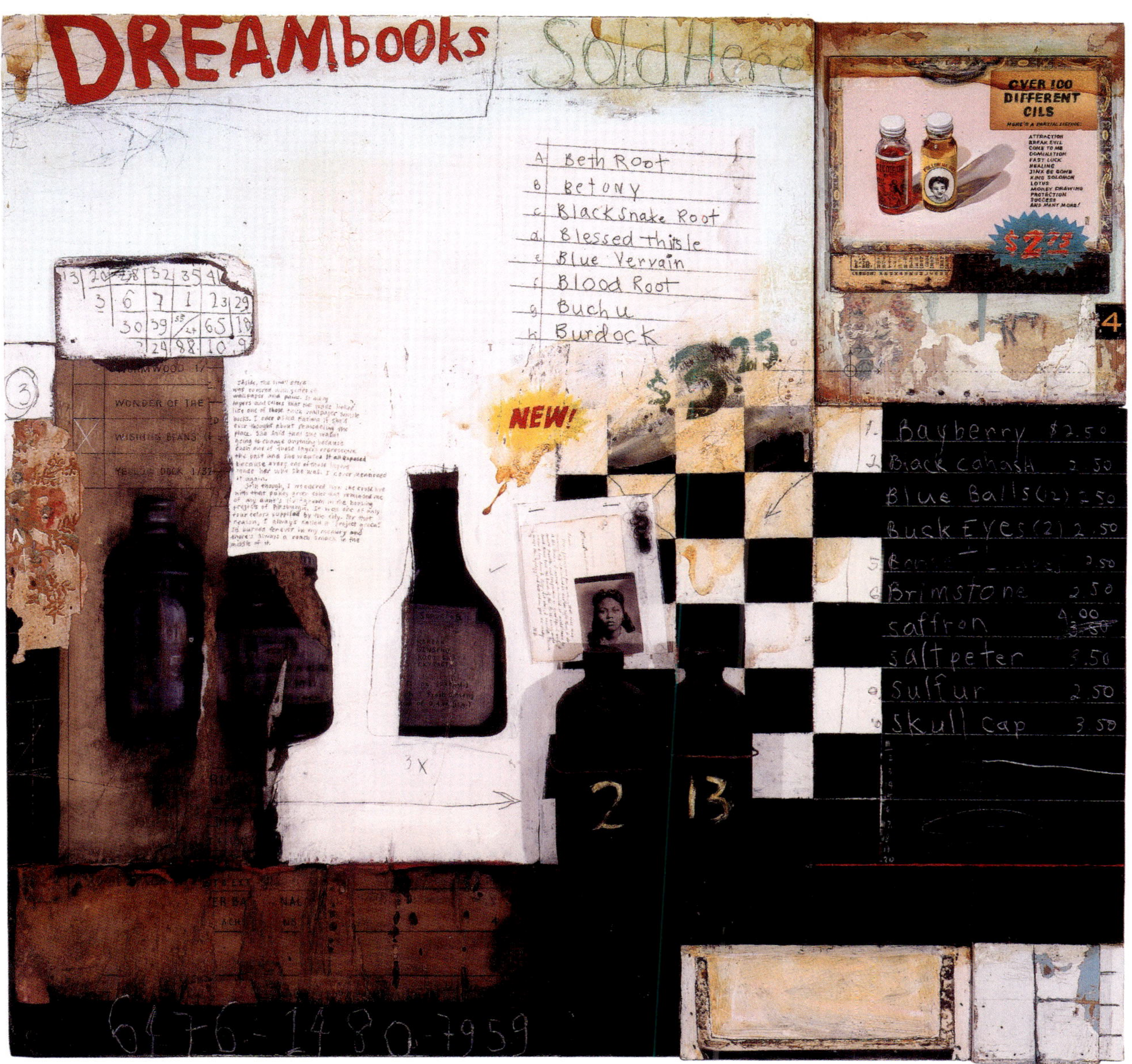

Dreambooks 2001-02

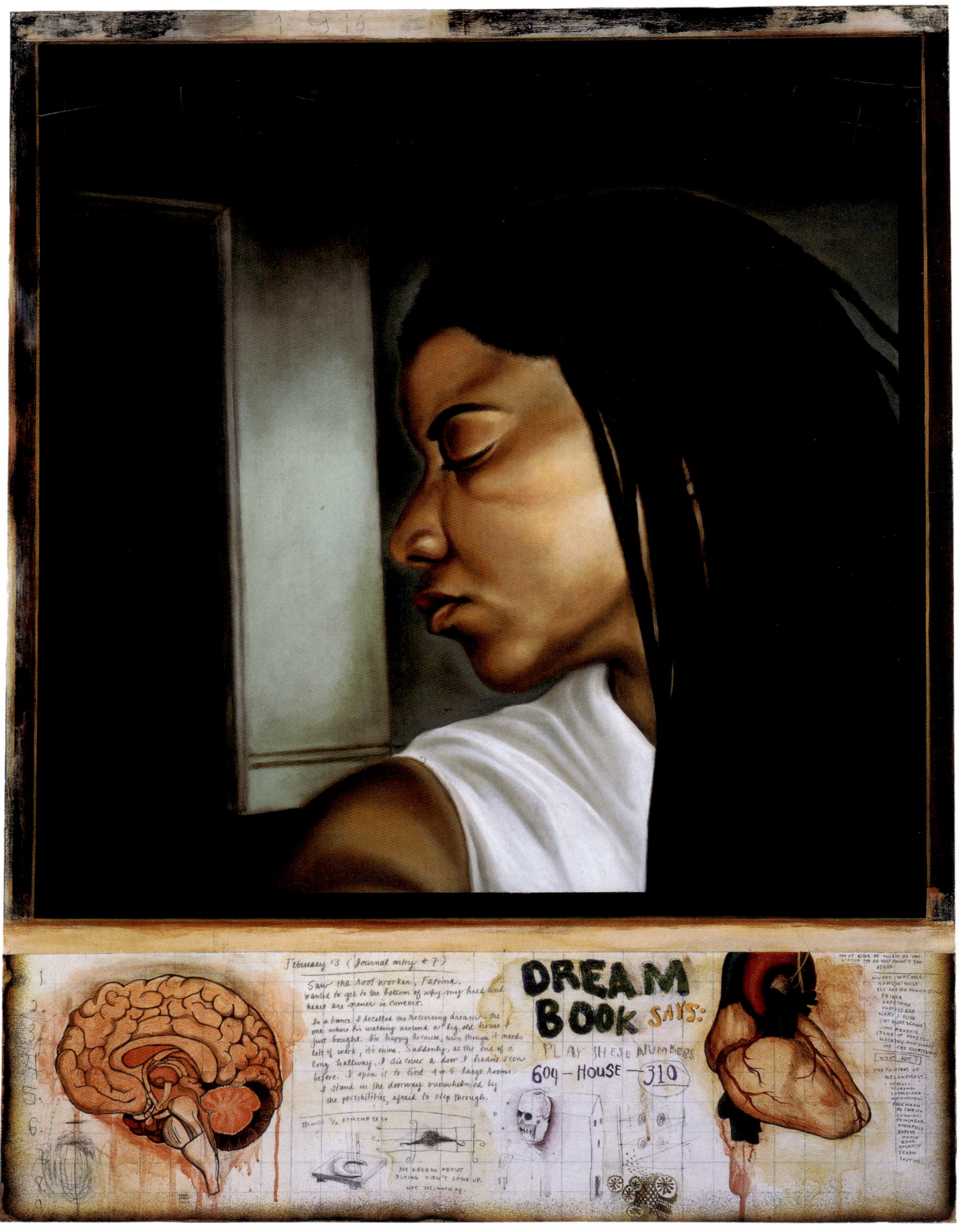
February 13 (Journal entry #7)
Saw the root worker, Fatima.
wanted to get to the bottom of why my head and heart are never in concert.
In a trance I recalled the recurring dream - the one where I'm walking around a big old house I just bought. I'm happy because, even though it needs lots of work, it's mine. Suddenly, at the end of a long hallway, I discover a door I hadn't seen before. I open it to find 4 or 5 large rooms. I stand in the doorway overwhelmed by the possibilities, afraid to step through.
MY DREAMS ABOUT FLYING DIDN'T COME UP. NOT YET, ANYWAY.
DREAM BOOK SAYS:
PLAY THESE NUMBERS
604 — HOUSE — 310

Renée Stout

Selected Solo Exhibitions

Mystery and Melancholy of the Street, David Beitzel Gallery, New York, 2000

Monotypes and Other Works, The Beach Museum at Kansas State University, Manhattan, KS, 2000

Rantings in the Night Studio, Morgan Gallery, Kansas City, MO, 1999

The Ranter, David Adamson Gallery, Washington, DC, 1998

Dueling Dualities, Steinbaum Krauss Gallery, New York, 1997

Recent Sculpture, Cline/LewAllen Gallery, Santa Fe, NM 1997

Madam's Secrets, David Adamson Gallery, Washington, DC, 1996

Dear Robert, I'll See You at the Crossroads: A Project by Renée Stout, University Art Museum, University of California - Santa Barbara, Santa Barbara, CA, 1995

Astonishment and Power: Kongo Minkisi and the Art of Renée Stout, National Museum of African Art, Smithsonian Institution, Washington, DC, 1993

Recent Sculpture, Pittsburgh Center for the Arts, Pittsburgh, 1992

Recent Sculpture, B.R. Kornblatt Gallery, Washington, DC, 1991

Chapel Gallery, Mount Vernon College, Washington, DC, 1987

Selected Group Exhibitions

2001

Personal Histories, Center for Documentary Studies, Duke University, Durham, NC

2000

The View from Here, State Tretyakov Gallery, Moscow, Russia

The Likeness of Being: Contemporary Self-Portraits by 60 Women, DC Moore Gallery, New York

1999

Secular/Spiritual Identities: The Blues, The University of Florida at Gainesville Art Gallery

Locating the Spirit: Religion and Spirituality in African American Art, Anacostia Museum and Center for African American History and Culture, Smithsonian Institution, Washington, DC

1998

The Next Word, Neuberger Museum of Art, Purchase College, State University of New York, Purchase, NY

Identity Revealed: Meaning and Message in Contemporary Art, Ackland Museum, Chapel Hill, NC

Crossing Cultures, Lewallen Contemporary, Sante Fe, NM

Resonant Forms: Contemporary African American Women Sculptors, Anacostia Museum and Center for African American History and Culture, Smithsonian Institution, Washington, DC

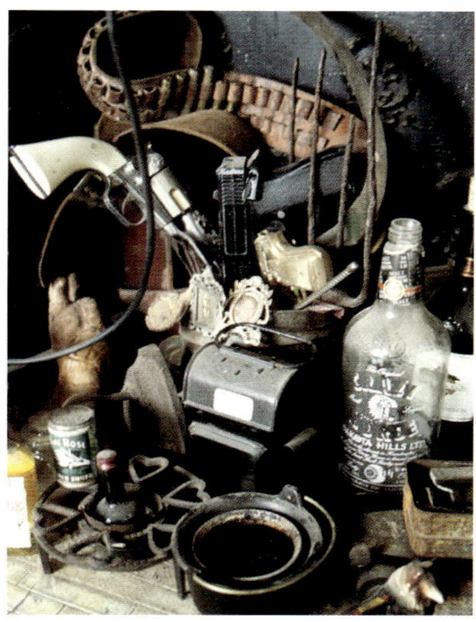

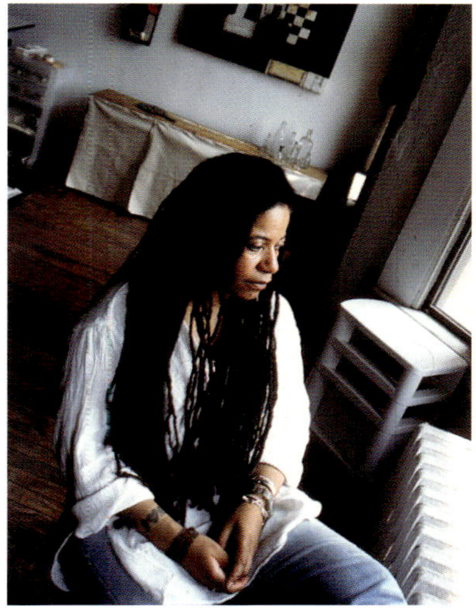

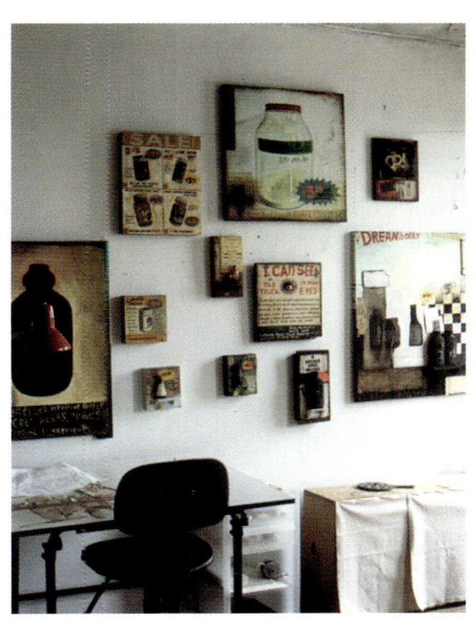

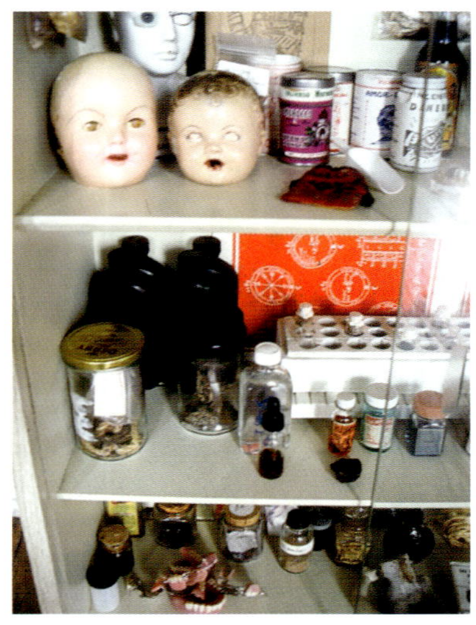

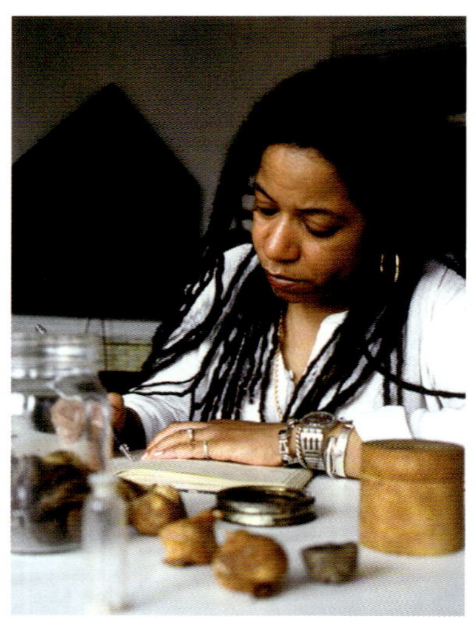

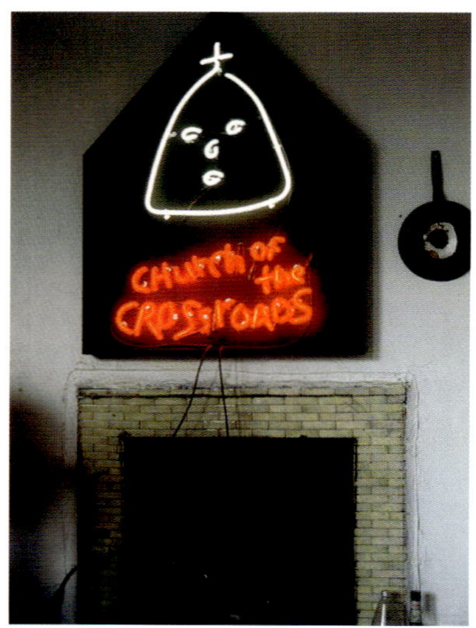

Postcards from Black America, De Beyerd Museum, The Netherlands

Seeing Jazz, Smithsonian Institution Traveling Exhibition Service, Washington, DC

1997

Searching for the Spiritual, Depree Art Center and Gallery, Hope College, Holland, MI

Pursuit of the Sacred: Invocations of the Spiritual in Contemporary African American Art, Betty Rymer Gallery, School of the Art Institute of Chicago, Chicago

Biennial Exhibition of Public Art, Neuberger Museum of Art, State University of New York, Purchase, NY

1996

Kaleidoscope: Themes and Perspectives in Recent Art, National Museum of American Art, Smithsonian Institution, Washington, DC

Wylie Avenue Juke and Effective Sight, College of Charleston, Halsey Gallery, Charleston, SC

My magic pours secret libations, Florida State University, Museum of Fine Arts, Tallahassee, FL

1995

Inside Visions/Outside the Mainstream, Horwitch LewAllen Gallery, Santa Fe, NM

American Color, Porter Troupe Gallery, San Diego, CA

Fetishism: Visualizing Power and Desire, The South Bank Centre, London, England, and traveling

1994

Small Works, David Adamson Gallery, Washington, DC

Sharing the Dream, Sangre De Christo Art Center, Pueblo, CO

Metaphysical Metaphors, High Museum of Art, Atlanta, GA

Artist's Sketchbooks, National Museum of Women in the Arts, Washington, DC

Free Within Ourselves, National Museum of American Art, Smithsonian Institution, Washington, DC

Luxor v1.0, Corcoran Gallery of Art, Washington, DC

1993

Ideo-syncretics 2: Diasporic Creolizations, Cavin-Morris Gallery, New York

Collectibles, The LewAllen Gallery, Sante Fe, NM

Touch: Beyond the Visual, Hand Workshop, Richmond, VA

1992

LewAllen Gallery, Sante Fe, NM

The Migrations of Meaning, INTAR Hispanic American Arts Center, New York

Sites of Recollection: Four Altars and a Rap Opera, Williams College Museum of Art, Williamstown, MA

Houses of Spirit/Memories of Ancestors, Bronx Council on the Arts at Woodlawn Cemetery, Bronx, NY

Homeplace, Henry Street Settlement/Louis Abrons Arts Center, New York

Image, Object, Memory, Hand Workshop, Richmond, VA

Present Tense, University of Wisconsin-Milwaukee Art Museum, Milwaukee, WI

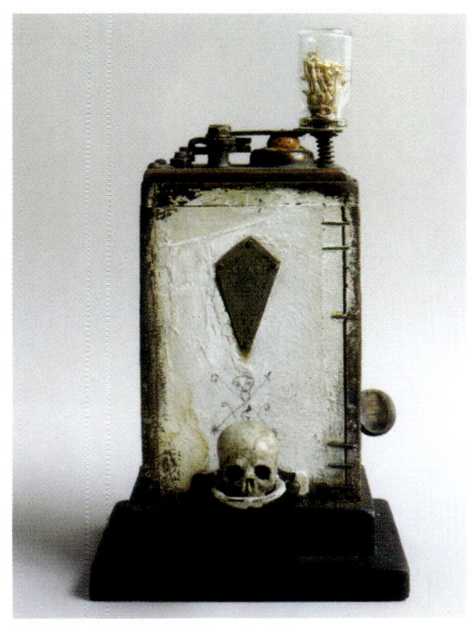

1991

Site-seeing: Travel and Tourism in Contemporary Art, Whitney Museum of American Art Downtown at Federal Reserve Plaza, New York

Power and Spirit (Renée Stout: Spirit House #2 ; Fred Wilson: The Other Museum), Washington Project for the Arts,Washington, DC

1990

Gathered Visions: Selected Works of African-American Women Artists, Anacostia Museum and Center for African American History and Culture, Smithsonian Institution, Washington, DC

Selected Bibliography

Collins, Lisa Gail, *The Art of History: African American Women Artists Engage the Past* (2002) pp., 60, 62-63.

Valdez, Sarah, "Renée Stout at David Beitzel," *Art in America*, (January 2002) pp. 111-112.

Oguibe, Olu, *Fresh Cream* (10 Curators and 100 Artists, published 2000), Renée Stout, p. 586.

Barnes, Denise, "Sculpting Political Issues," *The Washington Times*, April 3,1999, B1

Protzman, Ferdinand, "Renée Stout's `O' St. Blues," *The Washington Post*, Oct. 8, 1998, D5

Goodman, Jonathan, "Renée Stout," *Art In America*, v. 86 (January 1998), p. 94

Protzman, Ferdinand, "Through a Glass Darkly," *The Washington Post*, Nov. 2, 1996, C1

Days-Serwer, Jacqueline, "American Kaleidoscope: Themes and Perspectives in Recent Art," National Museum of American Art, (1996): pp. 11-12

Roscoe-Hartigan, Linda, "Renée Stout" (*American Kaleidoscope: Themes and Perspectives in Recent Art*), National Museum of American Art, 1996: pp. 52-59

Berns, Marla C. and George Lipsitz, "Dear Robert, I'll See You at the Crossroads: A Project by Renee Stout", University Art Museum, University of California, Santa Barbara, CA.

Gibson, Eric, "Inspiration Drawn from One's Roots: Renee Stout Updates African Styles," *The Washington Times*, May 9, 1993, D4

Harris, Michael, "The Art of Renée Stout," *Astonishment and Power*, Washington, D.C.: National Museum of African Art, Smithsonian Institution, (1993), catalogue

James, Curtis, "Astonishment and Power: Kongo Minkisi and the Art of Renee Stout," *Art News*, v. 92 (October 1993), p. 171

Mandle, Julia Barns, and Deborah Menaker Rothschild, eds., "Sites of Recollection: Four Altars and a Rap Opera" (Williamstown Massachusetts: Williams College of Art, 1992)

Plagens, Peter, "Africa Meets the West," *Newsweek*, February 19, 1990, p. 68

Rubenfeld, Florence, "Renée Stout," *Arts Magazine*, May 1991, p. 79

Thompson, Robert Farris, Illuminating Spirits in *Astonishment and Power*, National Museum of African Art, *African Arts*, v. 26 (1993): pp. 61-69;

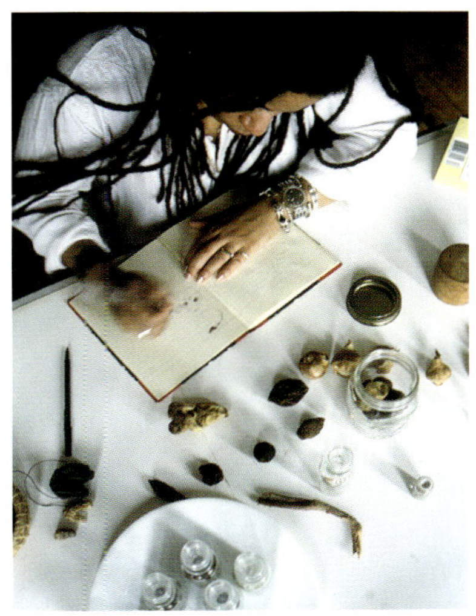

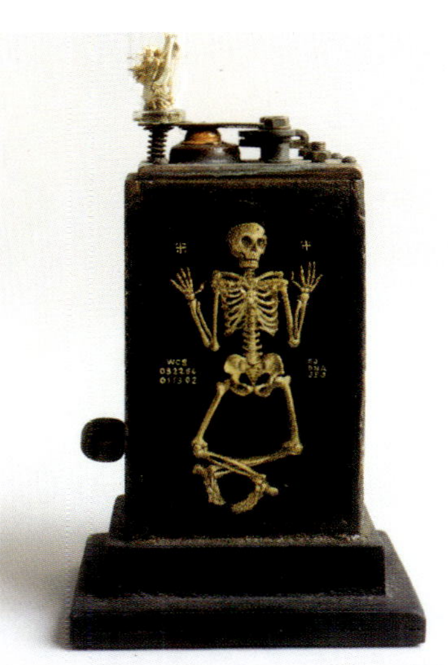

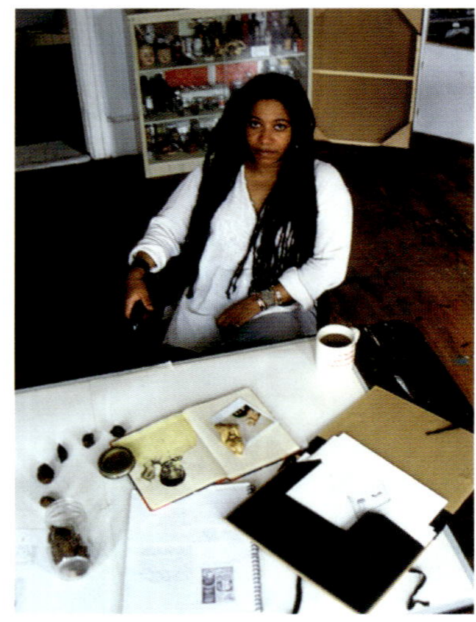

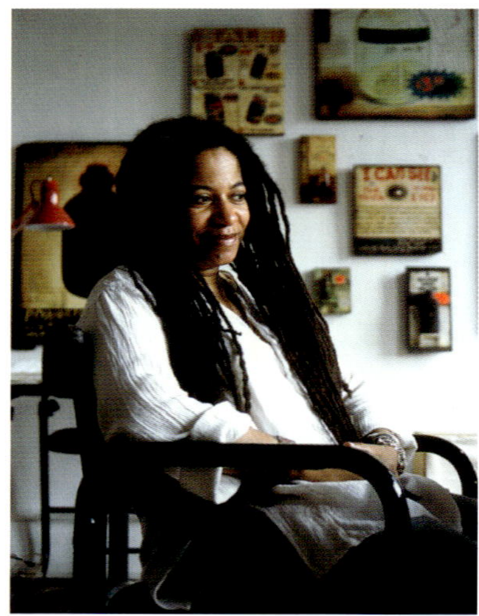

Thompson, Robert Farris, **Betye and Renee: Priestesses of Chance and Medicine**, *The Migration of Meaning* (New York: INTAR Gallery, 1992)

Wardlaw, Alvia, Robert V. Rozelle, and Maureen A. McKenna, eds., **"Black Art/Ancestral Legacy: The African Impulse in African-American Art,"** (Dallas, Dallas Museum of Art, 1989)

Collections

Ackland Art Museum, Chapel Hill, NC

Allegheny Community College, Pittsburgh

Baltimore Museum of Art, Baltimore, MD

The Corcoran Gallery of Art, Washington, DC

Dallas Museum of Art, Dallas

Memorial Art Gallery, Rochester, NY

National Museum of American Art, Washington, DC

Tucson Museum of Art, Tucson, AZ

University Art Museum, University of California at Santa Barbara, Santa Barbara, CA

The Virginia Museum of Fine Arts, Richmond, VA

Grants and Fellowships

2000, Residency, Tryon Center for Visual Art, Charlotte, NC

1999, Pollock Krasner Foundation Award

1999, Anonymous Was a Woman Award

1997, Mayor's Art Award (For Excellence in an Artistic Discipline, Washington, DC)

1993, The Mid Atlantic Arts Foundation, National Endowment for the Arts, Regional Visual Arts Fellowship (sculpture and crafts)

1993, The Louis Comfort Tiffany Foundation Award

1991, The Pollock Krasner Foundation Award

1984, Artist-in-Residence, Afro-American Master Artist in Residency Program (six-month residency), Northeastern University, Boston, 1984-85

Teaching Experience

University of Georgia, Athens, Visiting Professor, 1995
Spring quarter, graduate painting and undergraduate painting

Panels

1999, D.C. Commission on the Arts and Humanities (Visual Art)

1998, Pew Fellowships in the Arts, Philadelphia

1995, National Endowment for the Arts, Organizations and Publications

1993-94, D.C. Commission on the Arts and Humanities (Visual Arts)

Education

B.F.A., Carnegie-Mellon University, Pittsburgh, 1980

page: 83
Nipper in a Trance 2002

pages: 84, 85, 86, 87
Renée in Her Studio 2001

page: 84
Renée's Studio 2002

page: 85
Church of the Crossroads (neon) 1999

pages: 84, 85
Source Material 2000

page: 86
Ghede Object 2002
front & back

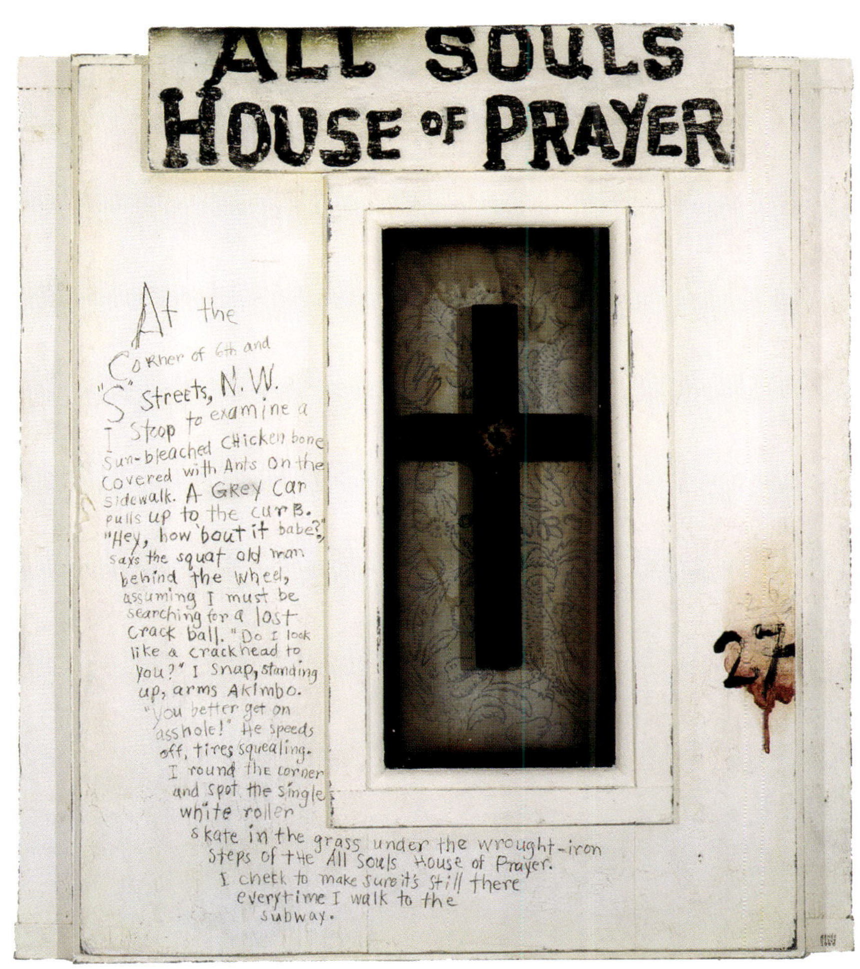

All Souls House of Prayer 2001

Checklist

All dimensions are in inches, height by width by depth. All works, unless otherwise noted, belong to the collection of the John and Maxine Belger Foundation.

All photographs by Dan Wayne, unless otherwise noted.

Still Life Untitled 1984
Acrylic. 18 1/2 x 24 1/2 in.
page: 4

No Self Bagging 1984
Acrylic. 21 1/2 x 23 5/8 in.
page: 5

Maull it! (Pittsburgh Still life) 1985
Acrylic on canvas. 24 x 30 in.
page: 6

Fate Line 1987
Mixed media. 48 1/2 x 68 3/4 in.
Collection of Sara Stout
photo by Greg Staley
page: 8

Untitled 1987
Acrylic. 30 1/2 x 30 1/2 in.
page: 21

Self-Portrait 1988
Acrylic on canvas. 44 x 55 in.
Collection of the artist
photo by Greg Staley
page: 9

Fetish #2 1988
Mixed media. 64 in. h.
photo courtesy of Dallas Museum of Art
(not in exhibition)
page: 19

Face Pouch 1990
Mixed media. 5 1/4 x 12 x 6 1/4 in.
Private Collection
photo by Franko Khoury
(not in exhibition)
page: 10

She Kept Her Conjuring Table Very Neat 1990
Mixed media
Private collection
photo by Ed Owen
(not in exhibition)
page: 70

Traveling Root Store 1993
Mixed media. 36 x 34 x 15 1/2 in.
photo by Renée Stout
(not in exhibition)
page: 35

Love Charm #2 1994
Mixed media. 9 x 8 x 7 in.
page: 39

Point of View 1994
Photo and mixed media. 28 1/2 x 18 x 10 in.
pages: 42 & 45

Traveling Root Store #2
(Madam Ching Goes High Tech) 1994
Mixed media. 21 5/8 x 24 x 19 1/4 in.
page: 40

When it Comes to Love, Elegba the Trickster Dangles a Carrot in Front of My Face, 1994
Mixed media. 42 x 12 x 13 in. carrot 13 in.
page: 27

Man Trap 1994 - 1995
Mixed media. 24 3/8 x 28 x 73 3/4 in.
pages: 11-12

Madam Ching's Love Products 1995
(from Madam Ching's Museum of Love installation)
Mixed media. 64 x 22 1/8 x 17 1/4 in.
page: 36

Two Secret Society Passports 1995 - 1996
Mixed media. 12 x 10 1/2 x 4 in.
page: 59

Conjuring Vest 1996
Mixed media. 28 x 17 x 4 in.
pages: 37-38

Bobby Hutton
(from *Arsenal for the Fire Next Time*) 1997
Mixed media. 5 x 6 1/2 x 1 in.
page: 52

The Chairman Watching the Game 1997
Mixed media. Dimensions vary
page: 50

Che Guevara
(from *Arsenal for the Fire Next Time*) 1997
Mixed media. 6 1/8 x 9 x 1 3/8 in.
page: 52

Geronimo
(from *Arsenal for the Fire Next Time*) 1997
Wood, metal. 10 x 14 x 2 1/2 in.
page: 52

Harriet Tubman
(from *Arsenal for the Fire Next Time*) 1997
Mixed media. 11 x 13 x 3 1/2 in.
page: 52

Headstone for the Gang of 8 1997
Mixed media. 63 x 22 x 9 1/2 in.
page: 49

John Brown
(from *Arsenal for the Fire Next Time*) 1997
Wood, metal, screws. 5 x 8 1/2 x 1 1/2 in.
page: 52

My Door 1997
Mixed media. 79 x 28 1/2 x 5 in.
page: VII

My Secrets Keep Me Going 1997
Mixed media. 12 1/2 x 5 x 5 in.
page: 13

Process of Disassociation 1997
Mixed media. 18 x 33 x 6 1/2 in.
Private Collection
photo by Becket Logan
(not in exhibition)
page: 46

Red Room at 5:00 (portfolio of six) 1997 - 99
Cibachrome prints. 11 x 14 in.
concept & staging by artist, photos by Renee Stout & Gary Lilley
pages: 41-42

Sign from Grandma Bea's Church 1997
Mixed media. 36 1/4 x 20 x 3 3/16 in.
page: 66

Song of the Cicada 1997
Mixed media. 53 x 80 x 10 in.
Private Collection
photo courtesy of Bernice Steinbaum Gallery
(not in exhibition)
page: 62

26 Whispers 1997
Mixed Media. 15 x 9 x 5 in.
page: 14

At the Gate of Kalfou 1998
Acrylic and mixed media on wood. 30 x 28 x 3 in.
pages: 28 & 47

Baby's First Gun 1998
Mixed media and toy gun. 6 x 7 x 5 in. (open)
page: 54

Between Midnight and Day 1998
Mixed media. 5 x 18 x 16 in.
page: 15

Carpetbagger Politician Goes for Free Ride on Homeless Woman 1998
Mixed media. 36 x 20 x 20 in.
page: 48

Conspiracy Theory 1998
Mixed media. 14 x 11 x 11 in.
page: 58

Harriet Carried a Gun Like This 1998
Watercolor and collage on paper
mounted on wood. 7 1/2 x 28 in.
page: 53

Hoo Doo'd (to Jesse Helms) 1998
Mixed media. 36 x 27 3/4 x 4 in.
page: 56

Hustler's Icon 1998
Mixed media. 12 x 10 x 4 in.
page: 55

Juke Joint Window 1998
Mixed media. 33 1/2 x 23 1/2 x 3 in.
page: XI

The Lovers 1998
Stuffed birds, cage, beads, lace, dirt. 14 x 19 x 10 in.
page: 69

Mantle in a House of Ogún 1998
Mixed media. 18 1/2 x 29 x 1 3/4 in.
page: 29

Oath to Ogún 1998
Mixed media. 28 x 40 1/2 x 3 1/2 in.
page: 30

Ogún's Bed 1998
Wire, found objects. 10 x 72 x 48 in.
page: 31

Soul Saving Center #3 1998
Mixed media. 100 x 48 x 18 in.
page: 67

Winnie Mandela II
(from *Arsenal for the Fire Next time*) 1998
Wood, metal. 11 x 13 x 3 1/2 in.
page: 52

Church of the Crossroads 1999
Neon and wood wall construction
52 x 37 x 3 in.
page: 16

Dancing with Demons 1999
Mixed media
21 x 17 1/4 in.
page: 57

Kinley's Drug Store 1999
Mixed media. 23 3/8 x 21 3/4 x 1 3/4 in.
page: 34

Ranting in the Night Studio 1999
Mixed media. 36 1/2 x 63 1/2 x 1 3/8 in.
page: 60

We Do Tattoos 1999
Mixed media. 26 1/4 x 20 1/2 in.
Cover & detail page: I

All Souls House of Prayer 2000
Mixed media. 28 3/4 x 25 x 2 1/4 in.
page: 65

All Souls House of Prayer 2000
Mixed media. 28 1/4 x 22 5/8 x 2 5/8 in.
Collection of the artist
photo by Greg Staley
page: 88

Come See Me 2000
Mixed media. 32 x 24 x 1 in.
page: 33

Cures 2000
Mixed media. 17 15/16 x 17 15/16 x 3 1/8 in.
page: 23

Healer, Heal Thyself 2000
Oil, acrylic on wood. 36 x 36 in.
Collection of the artist
photo by Greg Staley
page: 81

Hoodoo Holy 2000
Mixed media. 13 1/2 x 11 5/8 x 2 11/16 in.
page: 2

I Can Heal 2000
Neon sign and five mixed media objects.
28 1/2 x 36 1/2 x 5 in.
page: 17

Legba's Lesson Learned 2000
Mixed media. 37 x 36 in.
page: 26

Packet Kongo 2000
Oil, mixed media on wood. 12 x 10 in.
Collection of the artist
photo by Greg Staley
page: IX

Storefront Church, Georgia Avenue 2000
Mixed media. 48 x 48 in.
Collection of the artist
photo by Greg Staley
page: 80

Amor II 2001
Acrylic & mixed media on wood panel. 8 x 7 1/4 in.
Collection of the artist
photo by Greg Staley
page: 76

Dreambooks 2001-2002
Mixed media. 32 x 33 x 2 1/2 in.
Collection of the artist
photo by Greg Staley
page: 82

Seat of Power 2001
Mixed media. 36 x 21 x 21 in.
page: 61

Hoodoo Holy Water 2001
Mixed media. 13 1/4 x 6 3/4 x 3 1/2 in.
Collection of the artist
photo by Greg Staley
page 73

Liver, Stomach, Pancreas 2001
Mixed media. 7 x 5 1/2 x 3 in.
Collection of the artist
photo by Greg Staley
page: 75

The Scream at 42 2001
Acrylic/oil on board. 36 x 36 in.
photo by Greg Staley
page: 63

See the Truth 2001
Mixed media on wood. 14 x 13 x 2 in.
Collection of the artist
photo by Greg Staley
page: 79

Store Front Church 2001
Acrylic on board. 48 x 48 in.
page: III

Three Wise Men 2001
Mixed media. 10 1/2 x 5 3/8 x 2 1/2 in.
Collection of the artist
photo by Greg Staley
page: 74

Two for Five 2001
Acrylic, spray paint on wood. 17 x 14 in.
Collection of the artist
photo by Greg Staley
page: 72

Fatima's 2002
Acrylic & mixed media on wood. 36 x 48 in.
Collection of the artist
photo by Greg Staley
page: 71

Ghede Object 2002
Mixed Media. 8 3/4 x 4 3/4 x 5 in.
Collection of the artist
photo by Greg Staley
page: 86

Jinx Killer Bath 2002
Oil and mixed media on wood. 24 x 24 in.
Collection of the artist
photo by Greg Staley
page: 77

Mandingo Bitters 2002
Acrylic, mixed media on wood. 23 x 8 3/4 in.
Collection of the artist
photo by Greg Staley
page: 74

Nipper in a Trance 2002
Oil, acrylic, mixed media. 48 x 36 in.
Collection of the artist
photo by Greg Staley
page: 83

Power & Luck 2002
Acrylic & mixed media on wood. 32 1/2 x 24 in.
Collection of the artist
photo by Greg Staley
page: 78